YOU ARE NOT ALONE

You Are Not Alone

Copyright © 2020 by Roger D. Blackwell, Ph.D.
All rights reserved.
This book is protected under the copyright laws
of the United States of America. This book may not be copied
or reprinted for commercial gain or profit.
Union Hill is the book publishing imprint of The Center for Executive Leadership,
a 501(c)3 nonprofit organization.

All Scripture quotations, unless otherwise indicated, are taken from the New
American Standard Bible (NASB). Copyright 1995 by The Lockman Foundation.

Union Hill Publishing
200 Union Hill Drive, Suite 200
Birmingham, AL 35209

www.rogerblackwellbusiness.com

1 2 3 4 5 6 7 8 9 10

Printed in the United States of America

YOU ARE NOT ALONE

And Other Lessons a Teacher
Learned from Parents,
Professors,
and 65,000 Students

ROGER D. BLACKWELL, PH.D.

OTHER BOOKS BY ROGER D. BLACKWELL

Saving America:
How Garage Entrepreneurs Grow Small Firms into Large Fortunes

Consumer Behavior, 10th edition
(Available in multiple languages and Asian editions)

Consumer Driven Health Care

Brands That Rock:
What Business Leaders Can Learn from the World of Rock and Roll

Customers Rule! Why the E-commerce Honeymoon is Over and Where Winning Businesses Go from Here

From Mind to Market

From the Edge of the World:
Global Lessons for Personal and Professional Prosperity

Global Marketing: Perspectives and Cases

Contemporary Cases in Consumer Behavior

Cases in Marketing Management and Strategy

Consumer Attitudes Toward Physicians and Malpractice

A Christian Approach to Transcendental Meditation

Strategic Marketing

Laboratory Equipment for Marketing Research

Research in Consumer Behavior

Cases in Consumer Behavior

To Linda

TABLE OF CONTENTS

1. Was It a Miracle Birth? — 1
2. Child Labor — 7
3. From Farmer to Entrepreneur — 15
4. The Downs and Ups of College Education — 25
5. What I Discovered in Graduate School — 37
6. Dusty and a Guardian Angel — 49
7. Go Bucks! — 53
8. FCI Morgantown — 64
9. Beyond Y2K — 75
   Roger's Rule for Success — 88
10. Take My Hand — 89
11. Conclusion: You Are Not Alone — 101

YOU ARE NOT ALONE

MOTHER AND FATHER were extraordinary parents. Their marriage of 73 years allowed a very ordinary child to learn life-changing lessons. It is miraculous that I escaped alive some of the events that happened over many decades. When people heard narratives of these events, they frequently commented, "You should write a book about what happened."

So, I did. For you.

My hope is you find examples from ways my parents influenced me that will be helpful in your own life.

CHAPTER ONE

Was It a Miracle Birth?

WHAT WAS the first event as a child you remember today? Take a moment to think about that. What age were you? What was that event, and what do you remember about it? For many, it probably happened at around age three or four, as it did for me.

The most vivid event for me, however, was one I cannot personally recall but heard about many times from my parents. It was my birth. No doubt you cannot remember your birth either, but maybe your parents told you some of the details.

Your mother probably remembers more about your birth than your father does. But my father knew and remembered more of the details surrounding my birth than my mother, because she was in too much pain to recall later what all was happening around her for about 20 hours when I started to be born in the tiny Ozark town of Weaubleau, Missouri.

It was my good fortune to hear my father tell the story of my birth over and over, often at Thanksgiving or Christmas. One December many decades later, he asked me what Christmas gift he could possibly get for a son who had a home, family, car, and good income. "How can I possibly find anything for you that you don't already have?" he asked.

After a few moments of reflection, I answered, "I would like a written account of the story of my birth, including details I don't know." Until the very end of his life, my dad could recall almost every detail of every year of his life, and he also was an engaging teacher and writer. I knew his narrative would be accurate and articulate.

That was my father's Christmas gift to me the year before I went to prison. The narrative later became part of the book he wrote in the final years of his life, *Farm Boy: Conditions and Incidents in the Early Life of a South Central Missouri Country Lad*. Rather than relying on me to tell a story I cannot recall, I offer the following pages—what he wrote in his own words.

Before we get to his words, however, I should tell you that it took my father, Dale J. Blackwell, 13 years to get a college degree after marrying his high school sweetheart, Rheva Allen, at age 18. Dale graduated from high school during the Great Depression, with a high school degree in "education." Missouri was one of the last two states to certify someone with a high school diploma to teach elementary school. He taught all eight grades in a rural one-room school, with a salary starting at $20 a month and an extra $2 a month as school janitor. This is how my father described their life.

> *"During the school year Dale concentrated on teaching, cutting (with Rheva's help) the winter supply of wood, and making educational plans. Dale planned to teach only two years and then go into business. However, he became fascinated with teaching and*

Chapter One: Was It a Miracle Birth?

decided to continue his education. The eight-month rural schools closed in April, allowing him to enter nearby Southwest Missouri State University for a full summer term of ten semester hours credit. Extra credit was given for higher grades, so he usually earned a few more hours than normal credit. When possible, he took extension classes offered evenings and Saturdays, taking courses that would eventually allow him to teach in high school, majoring in Business with a minor in Math."

Today, some students believe their parents should pay for a college education or they need loans to survive, but that was not the way poor people did it in the past. Dad's philosophy was "The difficult we do today; the impossible takes a little longer." It was a philosophy instilled in me by example if not by the genetics of my birth.

"The continuing depression and the lack of summer income made it tough financially. However, Rheva always found work wherever they were. One summer she earned 35 cents an hour at Sears when most businesses were paying 25 cents and hiring no new clerks. At a grocery store she worked long hours, first for 50 cents a day and later for $1 per day. When they saved (sometimes borrowed) $100, it would take them through the summer term at Springfield, the location of Southwest Missouri State. Their budget allowed $25 ($2.50 per week) for rent, $25 for food, $25 for education (tuition and books), and $25 for miscellaneous (travel, recreation, etc.). Another condition added to the financial squeeze. When Dale's salary had reached $60 per month, the District was short of money, so he had to teach half of the year without getting paid! However, every opportunity was used to add credits until the major event in their life, the birth of a son," as described in my father's own words from his book Farm Boy.

Birth of a Son

"Near the end of the summer term in 1940 a baby was expected. Dale and Rheva were living in a hot upstairs Springfield apartment with no air conditioning. Rheva's feet were swelling and she was very uncomfortable. A good friend on the faculty at Southwest Missouri State talked to the Chairman of the Business Division, Mr. J. D. Delp. He took Dale to the Office of the President and in his words stated: 'This man is expecting a baby and needs to take his wife home out of this God-awful heat!' The President asked what he could do. Mr. Delp said if he would write a memo to each of Dale's professors telling them to excuse Dale from the remainder of the term and the final examinations, he could take his wife home for the delivery. With a show of compassion, he wrote the memos and Dale was excused from each class.

Within two weeks, on August 7th, early morning, the time for delivery arrived. The family doctor, Dr. R. C. Nevins, was called. In less than an hour, he and his wife, a nurse, arrived. Rheva was in labor all day but could not give birth! With the help of Dale, his mother, aunt, and Rheva's mother, the doctor and nurse tried in vain forcibly to take the baby. Finally, in the evening, he threw the forceps across the room and said she had to be taken to the hospital in Humansville for a Caesarian section.

An ambulance was called and the only surgeon in the area, Dr. Stuffelbaum, was notified to be there with everything in readiness for the operation. Rheva was heavily sedated and examined with the conclusion of doubt in saving the baby, but they were going to try to save the mother! Dale could watch the entire operation and saw the lifeless form lifted out at five minutes to midnight! A frantic effort was made to get some sign of life, but to no avail. The forceps had stretched and cut

Chapter One: Was It a Miracle Birth?

the head, making it difficult to look at. The still lifeless form was laid away on a shelf as a 'still-born' infant. Then God brought forth a miracle!

After 40 minutes, Dale called attention of a nurse to what he thought was a slight movement of the baby. They started working with him, his heart started beating, and he started breathing! No sound was made until the next day, but he soon had the appearance and actions of a weak but normal babe. The parents were cautioned that there would likely be brain damage because of the long period of oxygen deprivation. Rheva's life was touch and go for several days, but Baby Roger Dale's life was stronger each day. There was never any Mother's milk, and because of the shortage of help in the small hospital, Dale could prepare and feed the formula around the clock and change diapers.

Because of Rheva's unstable condition, Dale never left the hospital. He had no money for eating out, so parents brought food and changes of clothes. Sleep for him in the hospital was a scarce commodity. Dale had saved back $20 for Dr. Nevins' home delivery fee but had to really depend on borrowing hundreds of dollars from several relatives just to get mother and babe dismissed from the hospital after 14 days. By scrimping and saving, and the raising of pigs and chickens, the hospital, the doctors, and all lenders were paid in full within two years. Because of her weakened condition, Rheva was unable to lift and care for the growing baby, and because adhesions almost caused her death, she had to spend additional time in the hospital. Finally, all recovered and were greatly blessed as a family."

The above words were written by my father, originally as a Christmas gift to me. You be the judge: Was I a miracle baby or not? But that is the reason my mother always called me her "miracle child." Because the delivery caused her to be unable to have additional children, she also referred to me as her "one and only." Years later I wondered, in addition to the doctor and nurse, my father and grandmothers, and me, was Someone else in that room?

I should also tell you that when my father told this story, often at Thanksgiving services at churches (because their anniversary was at Thanksgiving), he added the following words to the story.

"After his grandmother and I helped revive the disfigured baby that had gone without oxygen for 45 minutes, the doctor turned to me and said, 'That was a mistake because the baby will be severely brain damaged.'" Then my dad always added while chuckling in my direction, *"So his mother and I always wondered how Roger would have turned out if he were not born brain damaged."*

CHAPTER TWO

Child Labor

THE REST of the year of my birth and the following year were uneventful as my mother gradually regained her health and my father worked nonstop outside his teaching job to pay off bills from my birth. That all changed on December 7, 1941, described by President Franklin Roosevelt as a "Day of Infamy" because of the Japanese bombing of Pearl Harbor in the U.S. territory of Hawaii.

Like most men aged 18 to 50, my father registered and began military training to enter World War II. Although he completed training for the U.S. Army, his induction was postponed, probably because of my infancy and the delicate condition of my mother. But they wanted to join the war effort and do whatever they could to defend America. Again, from my father's own writing in the book *Farm Boy*, here is what happened.

"Remington Arms Company had a cost-plus contract with the government to produce small arms ammunition at the Lake City

Ordinance Plant east of Kansas City, Missouri. Thousands of workers were being employed to rush production. Dale started working at the plant six days a week. Rheva went to Springfield and checked Dale out of classes he was still taking. She sought and received some refunds on their payments for tuition.

Dale was assigned to work in the Engineering Division at Lake City in the hazardous area away from the main plant. In this area primer caps were filled with highly explosive powder. Dale kept time records of all maintenance engineers on each job they were assigned and was responsible for all tools and materials used by the engineers. He also arranged for specialists such as plumbers and electricians to come from other areas of the plant. He was amazed how the cost-plus system of operation caused so much waste. For instance, if a light bulb needed to be changed, two electricians came with a two-hour charge for each. If a one or two foot piece was sawed from a ten or twelve foot first-grade board that had been ordered, then the rest of the board had to be delivered to scrap. The Engineering Division, however, did have a slogan posted on placards that was impressive and stuck with Dale: 'The difficult we do immediately, the impossible takes a little longer," the philosophy that characterized his life.

"Dale liked the night shifts, especially the midnight to 8:00 shift. They added 5% or 10% bonuses and had less supervision. Having less to do at night, Dale started experimenting with machines—metal and wood lathes, milling machines, spring winders, etc. His foreman, Hugh Shaffer, encouraged him and put in a request to change his classification to machinist so his hourly pay rate could be increased.

This change in work assignment, however, led to a major injury that changed his life forever! There was a powder explosion that blew a chisel through his safety glasses and

Chapter Two: Child Labor

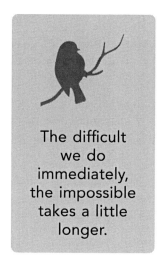

The difficult we do immediately, the impossible takes a little longer.

caused the loss of sight in the right eye. After several weeks in the hospital and at home, he returned to work and was assigned work away from the hazardous area. He was still in the Engineering Division and was responsible for writing orders to make or order machine parts and to keep the code records on all machine parts. He was put on salary, worked only days, and had less overtime pay. Because of the injury, the company offered to send Dale to its corporate office in Bridgeport, Connecticut, for special training and a lifetime position. However, he declined. But his physician warned him he should be prepared to live the rest of his life with a career that does not demand good vision or extensive use of his remaining functioning eye.

A family that works together stays together, and Rheva also worked much of the time at Lake City. This was a major help financially as Dale received only $20 a week for 108 weeks for the loss of sight in the one eye. Their work caused no problem for baby care as a 60-plus widow who was a friend of the family stayed with them, taking care of Roger, Dale, and most of the housework. That is the way World War II evolved. Everyone in the nation, whether young or old, black or white, rural or urban, in good health or not so good, eagerly did what he or she could for the good of the nation.

Roger loved his caregiver and called her 'Grandma Mag.' She was a 'jewel.'"

Years later, I joined with others to enlist Willard Scott to greet her on NBC's *Today* show when 'Grandma Mag' celebrated her 100th birthday.

The Blackwell family completed the War living in Independence, Missouri, a diverse urban area. The family of three (four with Grandma Mag) lived in a small second-floor apartment in what today is usually described as a distressed area of the city.

What's Your Blood Type?

Knowing your blood type could save your life or the life of someone else. My blood type is B negative, one of the least common, something my parents discovered when I was age 4. As an anemic kid, I had to swallow thick, black, terrible-tasting medicine, and for reasons I do not understand a physician recommended removal of my tonsils. Tonsillectomies have declined in frequency in recent years but were common earlier. After the operation, I spent the night in a hospital ward with a lot of other children. There were no private rooms or electronic monitoring stations in that Independence, Missouri, hospital, just a bunch of kids in beds with one nurse for the entire ward.

I remember my parents kissing me good night as they left my bed, but the next memory is my mother entering the ward the next morning, running to get a nurse to tell her "my child has turned white." I had been bleeding internally through the night and swallowing the blood. No one noticed until my parents arrived.

Hospitals during the war years did not stock much blood, certainly not B negative. Because of my father's time in the hospital earlier, he knew his blood type was also B negative. He rolled up his sleeve, and the nurse did a direct transfu-

Chapter Two: Child Labor

sion from his arm to mine, saving my life. Almost twenty years later in St. Francis Hospital in Maryville, Missouri, after my father experienced a heart attack, I was able to return the favor by donating my B negative back to him.

The St. Francis Hospital kept a register of people with Rh negative blood, and sometimes I would get a frantic call when a pregnant woman had a condition called Rh incompatibility. It occurs when a woman is Rh negative and her baby is Rh positive. One time when I was in college a call came in the middle of the night asking if I could report to the hospital immediately to donate blood. The streets were covered with ice and travel was treacherous, but I made it to the hospital and donated my B negative blood, hopefully saving the woman's life.

B negative blood can also be valuable I discovered when attending a few weeks of technical school in Dallas to complete final preparation and testing for an FCC license. The radio station where I worked paid my train ticket from Maryville to Dallas and rented the room I shared with other students, but I paid for my food. Up until that time in my life I had never eaten in a nice restaurant. I had eaten in diners with signs that said "Eat/Gas," but not a real restaurant. I wanted to celebrate completing the exam but had little money. Then I remembered, "I have B negative blood." After a few phone calls I found a blood transfusion office that paid $5 to donate blood, but $25 for B negative. That was my first steak dinner in a nice restaurant—and Dallas is about as good as it gets for steak dinners! I learned it pays to know your blood type, something I had discovered early in life.

The Farm Years

After World War II ended, life changed rapidly. My father,

13 years after beginning his college education, received his bachelor's degree from Southwest Missouri State, living out his philosophy that the "impossible" takes a little longer. Despite his physician's admonition not to choose a career that needed two good eyes, my father's major and minor were accounting and math, and he was offered a position teaching business courses at King City High School in Missouri. It was a minor miracle to be offered the position with no previous high school teaching experience. That is the good news. The bad news is that the salary was less than half of what he was making as a wartime factory worker.

Essie Ward in King City was a very imposing but kind woman who also was on the King City school board. In an era when few women had a law degree or CPA, she had both and controlled her family's farm, which was owned by Essie's brother, who lived in another state. She needed someone to manage the farm, and when she learned of my father's farm background, she let us live in the farmhouse rent-free in exchange for taking care of the family's cattle and crops. We had electricity but no central heat or running water. On hot summer and cold winter days in the outdoor privy, I learned why country folk appreciated catalogs from Sears and other retailers.

Living on a farm taught me an important rule: The only people in a farm family who do not work are those who do not want to eat. Child labor laws do not apply to farm children.

We raised almost all our food. My young friends and I worked in the farm gardens of our parents, plowing, weeding, and harvesting, and then snapping, washing, and preparing for my mother to can for the food supply that would last all winter. Children were also expected to help care for the chickens, and the feed sacks were always used to make clothes the farm children wore to school.

Chapter Two: Child Labor

Living on a farm taught me an important rule: The only people in a farm family who do not work are those who do not want to eat. Child labor laws do not apply to farm children.

King City was sometimes called the "Bluegrass Capital of America" because of the large fields of blue grass harvested in the area, usually with tractors and special harvesters. But those machines miss gullies and areas close to fences. My mother taught me how to use a "hand stripper" to gather the blue grass seeds from areas missed by the machines and then store the seeds in rows in an attic of the barn to dry before selling them by the burlap bag to a local seed company. It was hard, sweaty work in the latter part of the summer. But it was very lucrative for a six-year-old.

Also when I was about six, my grandfather gave me a baby pig. I took care of it until it grew large enough to sell for enough money to buy a U.S. Savings Bond, which later became worth $100.

Yes, I know there are abusive practices with child labor at various times in the history of the world. But I also know now that parents who teach their offspring how to work when they are children give them the great gift of the ability to support themselves as adults. Hard work makes people and nations prosperous.

As a child, I worked on the farm, cleaned chicken houses for other families (for good pay in high school), painted houses many times, harvested produce and animals and bought savings bonds. There were no food stamps or WIC programs back then. Through all my childhood work experiences, I learned why some people do well financially and others do not. From those early farm years, I learned the ***keys to success in life include diligence and work skills.*** Child labor teaches both, providing the gift of financial success as an adult.

CHAPTER THREE

From Farmer to Entrepreneur

LIFE ON the farm ended in the third grade, again due to the persistence and hard work of the man who believed the "impossible" takes a little longer to achieve. While teaching in King City, my father depended on my mother and me to manage the farm while he spent summers in Columbia, Missouri, to work toward a master's degree at the University of Missouri, which he achieved in 1948.

My father gave attention to each of his students, motivating some to achieve more than rural life provided. His students consistently won high school business contests sponsored by Northwest Missouri State College (NWMSC), about 40 miles from King City. As a result of his reputation as an excellent teacher and his recently acquired master's degree, the college offered him a position as Instructor in business. The salary was $1,400 per year, less than he made as a high school teacher but quite an achievement for a one-eyed guy who grew up on a rock-filled farm in the Ozark Mountains of the poorest county in Missouri. Opportunity for upward mobility, I read years later in Clayton Christensen's book *Prosperity Paradox,* is one of the essential attributes of how poor people and poor nations become prosperous.

Moving to the "big city" of Maryville (population then about 5,000) was traumatic for me. Everything was different, and I knew no one except my parents. We moved to a small house in the poorest area of Maryville, and I rode the bus each day to my new school. Financially, the only way for our family to thrive was my mother going to work at local retailer Montgomery Ward. Fortunately, when I arrived home from school on the bus, our next-door neighbor looked after me until my mother or father got home from work.

On the farm, we grew almost all our own food, my mother made my clothes from chicken feed sacks, and our family performed all household maintenance. In Maryville, we bought our food at a grocery store (but not restaurants because we didn't have enough money for that kind of extravagance until years later), and began to buy my school clothes from a retail store, usually Montgomery Ward since Mother received an employee discount. Even with both parents working, there was a constant shortfall between what my parents earned and what we needed for a middle class lifestyle.

When we bought things from stores, we contributed something to the economy I did not understand until several decades and graduate courses in economics later. On the farm, we had the goods and services we needed to live, but they were derived from what economists call "non-market production of goods and services." They contribute nothing to a nation's Gross Domestic Product (GDP) or income. When we buy the same things from a store, they are part of the GDP. That is important to understanding economic growth today in the United States and other countries because GDP

Chapter Three: From Farmer to Entrepreneur

growth is much higher when a nation transitions from an agrarian to an urban economy. Economists and politicians today who believe a nation can achieve GDP growth as high as in the past usually fail to consider why GDP growth is much higher when a nation is converting production of goods and services from non-market sources to manufactured, distributed, and retailed goods and services. People who believe U.S. economic growth in the future will be as fast as it was in the past have been spending too much time in Colorado! (Or Vancouver and an increasing number of places legalizing hallucinatory products.)

My first year in Maryville, my mother asked me, "Would you like to have a job?" My response: "That sounds like fun." With those words, I started my career as an entrepreneur and contributor to the nation's GDP.

With Mother's help, I responded to an ad for promoting greeting card samples from the New England Card Company and received sales materials and eight boxes of Christmas cards. With Mother watching from the sidewalk, I knocked on doors of neighboring houses asking if they would be interested in buying my greeting cards. Some said yes, and I sold all eight sample boxes for one dollar per box and soon ordered more. My second year went from sales of eight boxes to many more, and by age nine, my business was growing. My mother helped me open a Postal Savings account at the local post office, and after subtracting 10 percent to give to church, I saved most of the rest.

By the time I was 12, I was earning as much as the fathers of some of my friends in school and almost as much as my father. But when I was in ninth grade, our tiny family jointly decided my father should attend Missouri University to pursue a doctoral degree. I understood by then that he could never be promoted to a professor (with a professor's salary, much more than an instructor) unless he obtained a doctorate. This would be his first time to attend a university full time during the normal school year. It was also when I learned the lesson that the path to prosperity is upward mobility.

Dad took a two-year leave of absence (without pay), and we all moved to Columbia, Missouri. It was up to my mother and me to support the family so Dad could attend university. He achieved not only his doctorate but also an additional master's degree in accounting and statistics. Mother worked at a retail store in Columbia, and I became a paper carrier for the Columbia Missourian. It was there that I discovered the path to prosperity is also often a second job.

First, I obtained a position at the newspaper after school delivering large quantities of the paper (on my loaded-down bicycle) to racks in which customers deposited a nickel and took a paper. Since I paid only a penny a paper, my cash profits were good—but only if I estimated demand accurately at each rack because I lost a penny on every unsold newspaper. That work ended before 7 p.m., leaving time to work at a nearby Tastee-Freeze from 7 until 11 p.m. That allowed time to ride my bicycle home a block away, do my homework for school (sometimes) and be in bed by midnight. Fortunately, there were no videogames to distract me! Although I admit that sometimes I used a few of my nickels from the racks to play a pinball machine between my newspaper job and my dairy store job.

My parents taught me how to open a savings account, and I delighted in seeing it grow into a balance at first of hundreds and eventually thousands of dollars. My family was still driving an old Chevrolet that had seen better days after a decade of my father commuting between Maryville and Columbia. We desperately needed a new car, but after

Chapter Three: From Farmer to Entrepreneur

two years with no salary for my father, there was only one way to get a new car. I did what any child should do for parents. I loaned the total amount to my father to buy a new Buick. After he returned to Northwest State as a professor, he eventually paid all the money back. And on my 16th birthday, I took my driver's license test in a new Buick!

After returning to Maryville, I thought about restarting my greeting card business, but radio interested me. I bought a burned-out radio for 25 cents at a salvage store and rebuilt it. I liked music, both jazz and classical, and spent a little of my earnings buying records and a record player. While a student at Horace Mann High School, I hosted "Horace Mann Hits," a 30-minute program each week, at the local radio station. There I observed that the announcers had to dump trash and sweep floors after they finished a shift. That seemed like an opportunity for me. At an early age, I recognized **solving other people's problems is the key to success for entrepreneurs.**

Riding my bicycle to the radio station, I got an appointment with the station manager, Gil Posse, and suggested I could come to the station after school each day and clean the station—for free. He reflected a moment and responded, "That's a good idea, but you don't have to work for free. We will pay you 50 cents an hour." My career in radio (and eventually TV) was underway!

I learned all I could from the other announcers and the one engineer the station employed who explained a First Class FCC Engineering license was required to make repairs and adjustments at the station. I learned how to run the "board," cue up records on the turntables, and monitor the station's signal. Before long, when announcers wanted to run across the parking lot to King's diner to get a cup of coffee, they asked me to cover for them if the record ended before they returned. It was not long before I knew how to be a disc jockey. And a few weeks later, one of the announcers said he was going to party Saturday night and asked if I would cover for him to open the station on Sunday morning. (He knew that as janitor, I had a key to the station.)

"Glad to help," I replied, and my career as weekend announcer was born, often working 10- and 12-hour shifts. That did not interfere with my studies in high school, and eventually the manager asked if I would also like to work before school during the week as the police reporter doing live newscasts about the previous night's crimes. By the time I was a senior in high school, I was working nearly 40 hours a week, basically doing anything that needed to be done. And I was making nearly as much as some of the full-time staff. I used some of my income to buy a used car—for cash. I could have bought a nicer car with a loan, but I bought my first car and every other car during my lifetime the same way. Cars cost far less when you save the money first and buy with cash, instead of paying all that interest to someone else with money I worked hard to earn.

Learning about economics and business cycles was also part of my education while still a high school student. During a recession, the manager called all seven announcers together and announced he was going to have to lay off two announcers. I was not one of them. At the meeting, one of the other announcers jumped up and said, "How can you lay me off with three children to feed and keep Blackwell, who lives at home and saves all his money?"

The manager responded simply, "Because Roger is better than you." That was a pivotal moment in my education about economics, especially who survives recessions and how.

By the time I was a high school senior, I had advanced as a disc jockey and news announcer beyond my 50 cent

Chapter Three: From Farmer to Entrepreneur

starting wage as a janitor. But I realized engineers were paid more than announcers, so I enlisted the help of the Chief Engineer to show me how to repair the aging equipment of the station. He also told me that it was possible to get a First Class FCC license through correspondence courses. So, of course, I enrolled in a technical school and within a few years got my First Class FCC license while working at the station as a college student. The week before I received my engineer's license, the Chief (and only) Engineer took a better job in Kansas City and the manager made me the Chief (and only) Engineer. I had some scary times trying to keep a station on the air with only the knowledge from my correspondence course but somehow survived the four years in my evolution from janitor to Chief Engineer.

The ownership of the radio station changed, and I did not enjoy the same relationship with new management that I had with previous managers. Rather than comply with what I considered unreasonable (and unethical) requests of the new management, I quit. I was married by that time and needed a job. Fortunately, KFEQ, in nearby St. Joseph, Missouri, offered me a position as announcer, and eventually I progressed to work not only in radio but at its sister station, doing commercials and weekend weather on KFEQ-TV.

Child labor progressing into adult labor provides valuable lessons about the practical side of economics. One lesson is clear—when people focus on the prevailing "minimum wage," they miss an important point: Minimum wage should be called "starting wage." How much

Minimum wage should be called "starting wage."

an employee earns depends on what he or she does to progress beyond minimum wage. That is true even in corporations as large as Walmart, the largest corporation in the world. The current CEO, earning millions of dollars a year, started as a minimum-wage worker in a Walmart warehouse. Most of the top executives at Walmart, Wendy's, and other corporations started as minimum-wage workers. What they end up earning is determined by what they do themselves to increase their upward mobility. Employees do not get to the top by miracles; they get there by their own hard work and diligent efforts to improve their abilities.

My parents realized that an education includes much more than schools. When I was 8, they took me to see a parade in Bolivar, Missouri, where President Truman was dedicating a statue honoring Simon Bolivar. Waiting behind ropes with thousands of other people, I talked with the young lieutenant in charge of the troops guarding the ropes. It was a blistering hot day in July, and the Secret Service car just in front of the President's car stalled with a vapor lock, a term something only older readers will recognize. While security people were scurrying to get water to add to the radiator, the President's car was stopped, idling in the middle of the street. I darted under the rope, headed toward the President's car. A soldier stopped me, but the young lieutenant I had just met waved me on and I jumped up on the running board of the President's open Cadillac convertible. We chatted about 20 minutes until the Secret Service car was restarted and the parade moved on. It was a lesson about networking, learned at a young age.

Newspapers took pictures and wrote about me talking to the President, and I sent clippings of it to the White House. President Truman answered, thanking me. Over the years, the former President and I corresponded several times, so

Chapter Three: From Farmer to Entrepreneur

when I was a senior, I wrote him asking if he would be the graduation speaker for Horace Mann High School. I still have the handwritten letter from him saying his schedule would not permit him to accept. When I became a history major, I later learned President Truman probably made more historic decisions affecting the United States than any President since Lincoln. President Truman joined the Army instead of attending a university, but he was better educated than many college graduates as you can see from photos of the stacks of books in the Oval Office when he was President. My favorite quote by Truman is "Not all readers are leaders, but all leaders are readers."

My parents made many other contributions to my education. When Dad took a group of business students from NWMSC to visit the Kansas City Federal Reserve, he took me with him, and while lecturing to Dad's students, the Fed official allowed me to hold a $100,000 bill containing the picture of President Woodrow Wilson. (Yes, $100,000 bills do exist, but you will not find them at your local bank!) On another trip to Kansas City, my parents chaperoned a group of students and I accompanied them to my first opera (also their first, I believe). Porgy and Bess is still my favorite opera. These are the kind of experiences that great parents provide for children they want to learn the lessons of life.

Investor

Before we approach the end of this chapter, I should explain the second half of the chapter's title, Entrepreneur. I learned that what you have financially is not determined by what you earn as much as what you save. And I saved all my young life.

When I was still a teenager, I walked into the Nodaway Valley Bank in Maryville and asked Chilton Robinson, the

> I learned that what you have financially is not determined by what you earn as much as what you save. And I saved all my young life.

president (who was also one of my greeting card customers years earlier) if I could borrow $4,000. He immediately invited me into his office and asked why I needed $4,000. I told him I had saved $1,000 (this was after I loaned money for a car to my parents) and wanted to buy a house. He was concerned and asked if I was planning to leave home. I quickly said, "No, I want to buy a house and rent it." I showed him the real estate details of what I wanted to buy and my plan to pay back the loan from rental income.

Mr. Robinson made the loan to me, as a teenager without my father's signature as co-signer, and I bought the house, which did pay for itself with rental income. I sold it a few years later with the mortgage paid off, for several times my purchase price, which helped pay my way through graduate school with enough left over to make the down payment on my own house when I took a position at The Ohio State University. That experience taught me the value of being an entrepreneur. It also taught me the value of another lesson I learned from my parents: The first portion of what a person earns belongs to the Creator of the world that allows a person to prosper.

I believe in miracles, but financial success is not one of them. Nor is luck. ***"Miraculous" income and wealth is derived from diligence, hard work, and knowledge focused on opportunities for upward mobility.***

CHAPTER FOUR

The Downs and Ups of College Education

PEOPLE OFTEN believe a lot of money is required to obtain a college education. But that does not have to be the case. People who do not plan well or who make poor decisions about which college to attend pay a lot more than necessary to get an excellent education. Tuitions at colleges and universities vary from under $1,000 a year (or zero tuition with the right scholarships) to nearly $100,000 per year. Ask Siri about schools with lowest in-state tuition and even today you will receive a list of several with tuition less than $1,000 a year.

Even if the tuition is $10,000 a year, as a student you choose whether to pay $30,000 or $40,000 for your degree because you can usually complete a degree in three years (and sometimes less). All you need to do is take appropriate AP courses in high school, take one extra course per term (and most schools do not charge extra for that), and be careful about changing majors. That takes planning, of course, but people who fail to plan, plan to fail.

Paying for three years instead of four comes with a warning, however. If you choose three years to receive a four-year degree, you may not become as proficient in beer pong and other campus diversions.

Beneficial networking is a likely attribute of prestige schools, but the content taught at inexpensive schools is not fundamentally different from that at expensive schools. Attending an expensive university is much like buying a Mercedes, Porsche, or McLaren. If you or your parents want a $200,000 McLaren and have plenty of money you do not need for something else, it's okay to buy one. But a Ford or Chevrolet will get you to the same place for much less money.

Northwest Missouri State

Because my father finished his own education just prior to my starting college, no money was available for my parents to pay for my education at an expensive school. So, I attended a public college (now a university) in my hometown. The tuition was low (and still is at NWMSU), and I had a scholarship for half of the tuition. The most significant fact, however, was that I lived at home—saving thousands of dollars. My parents did not charge me rent, allowing me to finish my academic career without debt. That is one of the advantages of choosing a low-cost school near home.

The other way to make college affordable is to work at least part-time. I worked nearly full-time both of my last two years of high school and all years of college. And I did the usual college activities including fraternity, student government, and attending almost all football, basketball, and wrestling events. Almost all? You might question that assertion, but I was the public address announcer for all three of

Chapter Four: The Downs and Ups of College Education

those sports, so I rarely missed.

If you work while in college, you will be more attractive to employers than a student with a 4.0 GPA and no work experience. Over the years, employers told me they look for "jugglers"—students who know "how to keep a lot of balls in the air at the same time." Recruiters look for students who have significant work experience without sacrificing grades and campus leadership activities.

> If you work while in college, you will be more attractive to employers than a student with a 4.0 GPA and no work experience.

When describing how I managed to graduate from college without debt, I am not recommending all students do it the way I did, but my hope is to encourage anyone considering college without much money to realize that where there is a will, there is a way. Even for people without much money.

When I married during my junior year, I bought a mobile home with cash and sold it after graduation for only $50 less than I paid for it. That made rent free, except for the few dollars a month for a space in a trailer park. Although I did not pay much for my education, this excellent academic institution prepared me well enough to receive full-ride graduate scholarships at top universities, somewhat of a miracle for a "brain-damaged" child. It was not a miracle as much as frugality and careful planning, something to ponder when proposals are advanced to forgive students who accumulate a lot of debt in college. Is it socially responsible to reward students who fail to plan their finances carefully?

Even in programs such as medical school that are likely to generate large debt, there are "miracles" to help students who plan well. NYU Medical School recently announced all medical students will receive free tuition due to gifts of hundreds of millions of dollars by Ken and Elaine Langone, billionaires who shared the wealth they accumulated as entrepreneurs starting Home Depot. I hope they set an example that will be followed by other billionaires.

Opportunities exist for people who search diligently for them.

The Strongest Woman I Ever Interviewed

While I was a student at Northwest and working at KNIM, my duties included reporting local news, and the biggest news in Maryville in 1959 was the appearance of Eleanor Roosevelt, widow of former President Franklin Roosevelt, speaking at a special convocation for students and faculty of NWMSC. My assignment for the radio station was to cover her speech.

Mrs. Roosevelt was tall, well over 6 feet. She entered the auditorium wearing a hat, instantly grabbing the attention of everyone. Her voice was raspy, but resolute and vibrant, making every word seem so important that I should record it in my reporter's pad. Her theme was the need for a global perspective, a challenge for students of that day to be ready for tomorrow by understanding other countries' cultures. She also described her vision for a relatively new organization called the United Nations.

At the conclusion of the speech, I waited for her to leave by the back door of the Administration Building, which housed the auditorium in which she spoke. Other reporters were at the front door where she had entered, but because

Chapter Four: The Downs and Ups of College Education

Opportunities exist for people who search diligently for them.

I was also a student, I had an edge on other reporters by observing a limousine waiting at the back of the building and concluding she was leaving soon after the speech. Her plan was to leave immediately for a plane departing from the nearest large airport in St. Joseph, about 45 miles from Maryville.

As Mrs. Roosevelt exited the back door, I was the only one waiting for her. I approached her with my tape recorder, explained I was a reporter, and asked her if I could ask a few questions.

"I would love to talk with you," she said, "but I'm told I must leave immediately in order to be on time for the departure of my plane in St. Joseph."

I must have looked terribly disappointed, and perhaps she had some sympathy for the 19-year-old in front of her who looked more like a high school student than a reporter.

"If you want to ride with me in the limousine to the airport, I would be glad to answer your questions," she said, "but I don't know how you would get back to Maryville."

"Not a problem," I quickly volunteered and jumped in the back seat with her. I hitchhiked back home, something still possible in that era, but that is how I got one of the most historic interviews in my life. I learned a lot of lessons from that experience.

Her book *On My Way* had been published the previous year. That is probably the reason she was willing to travel to a remote spot in Missouri. Promotion of the book may also explain why she was willing for me to interview her. When an opportunity such as that offers itself, I have learned . . . take it.

Much of her speech and our conversation were about the need for planning in order to obtain success. "It takes just as much energy to dream as to plan," she said, encouraging people to plan if they hoped to obtain their dreams, whether those dreams were for a better life for themselves or for the world. About the only people who succeed in any worthwhile endeavor, I concluded, are those who plan to succeed. From that early interview, I formulated a belief that I related to students in my classes over the years. The way I stated that lesson as succinctly as possible was: If you fail to plan, you plan to fail.

If you fail to plan, you plan to fail.

Few people were as motivating as Eleanor Roosevelt. With every word she spoke came a compelling realization that I was in the presence of a woman who belonged to the world, not just to the United States. Indeed, her accomplishments involved the world as a delegate to the United Nations in 1945 and again from 1949 to 1952. She was a "teacher," not just for the students of NWMSC that day in Missouri but also for the world and for the ages.

Here are a few of the lessons I learned from Mrs. Roosevelt, in both her speech and my interview with her following the speech.

- **Compassion for the poor.** Today's society teaches young people the goal of achieving affluence. That message is repeated in every medium from rap music to best-selling books and prosperity preachers on

Chapter Four: The Downs and Ups of College Education

television, but Mrs. Roosevelt talked to youth about the need to dedicate themselves to the eradication of disease, starvation, and poverty. Only recently have I noticed her message of concern for the poor being echoed by some spiritual leaders such as Rick Warren, author of the Purpose Driven Life. He reminds readers that there are 2,000 verses in the Bible about concern for the poor. My own mission in life is to raise the average standard of living in the world, starting with an attack on poverty.

- **Compassion for minorities.** Long before "civil rights" was either a law or national priority, Eleanor Roosevelt demonstrated a concern for minorities. During World War II, the military was still segregated, but she went to an airbase housing the Tuskegee Airmen, the famed force of African-American aviators. Their funding was in danger of being withdrawn because of the bigotry of many toward "negroes," questioning their ability to "operate complex machinery." Mrs. Roosevelt gathered up the news media—including "movie news," the primary visual journalists of that era—went to the base, and flew in a plane piloted by one of the Tuskegee Airmen. Her words were strong about the need to overcome discrimination and bigotry; her actions were stronger.

- **Passion for a global perspective.** "Every student should study abroad," Mrs. Roosevelt told students at NWMSC, building on the experiences of some of the students in the audience who had already been abroad serving in the Korean War. She spoke about the need for strength in the United Nations and her experiences as a member of the Commission that helped draft and secure adoption of the Universal Declaration of Human Rights. She was effective in motivating me to think beyond U.S. borders for the first time in my life, a catalyst for my later interest in teaching "global thinking."

On the way to the airport, the tape in the recording machine ran for a little over 30 minutes, before it began flapping around the reel. I wished I had another tape, but we had few extra ones at the radio station in which I worked. Back at the station, I edited the tape and ran the story. My great regret is that I did not hold on to that tape for posterity. Instead, I put it on the shelf to be erased for use again the next day. But, of all the people I've met, few taught such indelible lessons as Eleanor Roosevelt. They can never be erased from my mind.

"Do you think the United States will ever have a woman as President," Mrs. Roosevelt was asked. It was a question asked of her often. I suspect the reason for the frequency of that question to her was the belief by many that Mrs. Roosevelt would have been as effective as President as she had been as First Lady, but the idea that being the wife of a former President would qualify someone to be President had not occurred to most people, at least back then.

The question about whether the U.S. would ever have a female President was a natural one, however, when it came to Eleanor Roosevelt. "Of course, we will," was her unequivocal and immediate response. Just several years short of 80, Mrs. Roosevelt died in 1962, leaving a legacy of lessons to be learned by every generation. Someday I hope to publish another book written while I was in prison but not yet published entitled *Lessons from Teachers*. It has a chapter on strong women I worked with over the years, such as Lady Margaret Thatcher, Secretary of State Madelyn Albright, and several female CEOs on whose boards I served. At the top of the list is Mrs. Roosevelt.

Perils of Being a History Major

History was the major I chose at Northwest for two reasons. First, I enjoy the study of history because I know that people who fail to learn the lessons of history are doomed to repeat it. Second, my plan was to be an attorney and history was highly recommended as a major to gain admission to law schools. That is why I majored in history at NWMSU—and perhaps a little bit because I knew history for me would yield better grades than math or science.

My enjoyment of history courses was matched by my admiration of the excellent professors who taught them. Admired them too much, as it turned out.

One of my professors taught that in all cultures and eras of history, people believe in something they call God. He argued this universal belief proves God is a creation of the human mind, not humans a creation of God. That made sense to me. Surely the professor was smarter than me because he was teaching me much about world history and cultures.

Another mistake I made was working so much that I did not have time to attend church or spend time studying teachings of the church. Many of my hours at the radio and TV stations were on weekends, often 10 or more hours at a stretch, plus commuting an hour each way when I worked at the St. Joseph TV station. I was too busy for church.

Believing there is no God simplifies things, although my sociology and psychology classes demonstrated religion often made important contributions to the establishment of universities, hospitals, and social welfare. Atheism seemed an easier choice. And if the smart professors whom I admired do not believe God exists, why should I?

In addition to my beliefs about God, my education also made a turn when I decided to transfer to the University of Missouri in Columbia. My wife, who had already graduated from Northwest, was admitted to a master's program at Mizzou and offered a teaching position providing a comfortable salary. I had completed all the required courses for a history degree at Northwest, only needing more total hours to graduate. When I talked to a Dean at the University of Missouri, he was optimistic about my admission to law school. I was also offered a good position at the newspaper where I worked while in high school. So, we literally hitched our modest 8-foot-wide mobile home to a truck and moved to Columbia, Missouri.

Mizzou

When my father attended Missouri during his doctoral program, I attended high school with the daughter of the Dean at MU Law School. He welcomed me to his office when I asked for advice about which electives I should take in my final year as an undergraduate. "Take every course in business you can. That is the future of law," he responded. And that is what I did, taking enough courses in that final year also to have a major in business.

But a funny thing happened on the way to law school. I really liked the business courses, maybe because my experience working at a newspaper and broadcasting stations and a few years in retailing gave me a practical understanding of marketing. I did well enough in their marketing classes that Dr. Wennberg and Dr. Shawver suggested I get a master's

Chapter Four: The Downs and Ups of College Education

degree in business and offered a full-ride tuition scholarship plus stipend if I did. Usually, that kind of assistantship was for Ph.D. students, but they made an exception for me and I accepted it. Everything paid to receive a master's degree in business sounded better than a partial scholarship I might receive in law school. All I had to do was teach a marketing class to undergraduates. What I learned from my professors at Missouri altered the direction of my life in ways I had not planned. Apparently, Someone had a different plan for my life.

It was not more than a few weeks into teaching the marketing class that I was hooked. Igniting the minds of students became my passion, and my professors began to encourage me to get a Ph.D. and pursue an academic career instead of law. So, I did.

It would have been easy to remain at Mizzou for a Ph.D., but a concerned professor said, "No, you should go to Harvard, where I went." Another encouraged me to apply to Wharton, where he graduated, and apply for the S.S. Huebner Fellowship. Dr. Wennberg, the professor who supervised my master's thesis, received his Ph.D. at Northwestern and offered to recommend me there.

Dr. Wennberg also provided a profound learning experience. A classically trained economist who retained his distinctly Scandinavian accent, he prodded me to write a thesis more the size and scope of a doctoral dissertation. He also enlisted Dr. William Stephenson from the Missouri Journalism School as co-advisor. Dr. Stephenson held two Ph.D.s, one in experimental psychology and one in physics. He was a general in the British Army during World War II, in charge of psychological warfare, and helped me develop statistical methodology using Q-sort factor analysis that, as I later learned, would have been appropriate for a Ph.D.

dissertation. Faculty members were impressed with what I was doing and instead of the normal defense in front of three professors, they scheduled an open defense attended by several professors and some of my M.B.A. classmates. This was my big show, but I barely completed typing the massive thesis and delivering it to Dr. Wennberg late the night before the defense.

After I finished presenting my results to this group of scholars, highly confident of what I had found, the first words of Dr. Wennberg in his Scandinavian accent were, "Vell, Mr. Blackwell, I am very, very disappointed in your work."

Dr. Wennberg, in front of the other professors and my fellow students, then proceeded to dissect my many mistakes, one by one. He was correct and exposed my carelessness in scholarly content on several levels. The other students and even some of the professors turned their heads toward the floor, embarrassed at my embarrassment. Dr. Wennberg was right, and I was wrong in handing him a thesis written in too few hours and without adequate checking on my part.

I learned more from that experience than if everything had gone well. Never again, I decided, would I go into a presentation as unprepared as I was in that master's examination. You learn more from your mistakes than your successes.

CHAPTER FIVE

What I Discovered in Graduate School

I DID NOT choose to be a teacher; teaching chose me. I respected my father's life as a teacher, but I wanted to be a dentist. My mother managed a store owned by a Maryville dentist who had no sons and liked my work in the store Mother managed for him. He offered to pay for my dental education if I would join his practice as he neared retirement. That plan hit a brick wall when I took a manual dexterity test consisting of carving something from a bar of soap. All I could create was a pile of soap chips, and the admissions director from UMKC Dental School suggested I consider a career depending more on cognitive skills than physical dexterity. That is why my plan as an undergraduate was to be a lawyer, a plan sidetracked by experience and business degrees.

Remaining at Mizzou would have been a comfortable way to get a Ph.D., continuing the assistantship I already had. In Columbia, I "knew the terrain," as strategy-guru Sun Tsu describes in his book *The Art of War.* Two incomes and nearly free rent in our small mobile home would have made a Ph.D. at Missouri an immediate and relatively painless path to a teaching career.

One of the best gifts in life is to be surrounded by wise people willing to tell you what you do not want to hear.

One of the best gifts in life is to be surrounded by wise people willing to tell you what you do not want to hear. That happened when several of the Mizzou professors said, "We would like to have you in the doctoral program, but you should not go into the academic world with all three degrees from the same school."

The professors were right. So, I applied to several universities with nationally respected doctoral programs in Marketing and travelled to St. Louis to take the Graduate Management Aptitude Test (GMAT) simultaneously with thousands of other aspiring graduate students around the world. Based partly on those scores, universities announced acceptance and scholarship grants on April 1.

I honestly thought someone had figured out how to play an April Fool's joke on me because on the first of April I received three letters all offering free tuition and fees plus stipends to enroll in their doctoral program. The annual cash was $3,600 at Northwestern, $4,000 at Harvard, and $5,600 at Wharton. That might not sound like much today, but in 1963, along with my wife's salary, it was certainly enough to live better than most graduate students.

Research ability is how top universities evaluate faculty, and any of those universities would have provided an excellent education in research methodology—the ability to make

Chapter Five: What I Discovered in Graduate School

decisions based on facts instead of opinions. For multiple reasons I will not bore you with, I chose Northwestern. That turned out to be an environment for the most important discovery any graduate student—or anyone, for that matter—can ever make.

The Great Train Escape

Northwestern is in Evanston, a suburb of Chicago, a big city for a Missouri boy to find a place to live. We looked at apartments in Evanston that would be near Northwestern, but when my wife was offered a teaching position at Lake Forest High School, several suburbs north of Evanston, we decided she should be close to her school and I would ride the train to Evanston each day. We found an apartment for $145 a month just a block from the train station in more affordable Lake Bluff, where a lot of teachers, firefighters, and city workers live adjacent to the very affluent suburb of Lake Forest. Lake Forest High School is a school where students often had names such as Armour, Swift, Field (as in Marshall) and other executives of major corporations.

You might be thinking it would be a burden to ride the train 45 minutes each way each day. It was the opposite. Riding the train provided time for the heavy reading assignments of Northwestern professors. The only negative (which was a positive for my health) was a one-mile walk from the train station to the NU campus on the shore of Lake Michigan. On cold winter days, I understood why Chicago, although named for its "wind-bag politicians," is also appropriately called the Windy City.

Sometimes I took the train to the campus in the morning, but in the afternoon rode part of the way home with Richard Lopata, who commuted to campus by car from his home in Highland Park. As a fellow marketing Ph.D student, he and I discussed classes we took together before dropping me at the Highland Park station so I could catch the next train to Lake Bluff, which also stopped at Highwood and Lake Forest. A conductor was usually in each car to sell the ticket to Lake Bluff.

On one cold and eventful day, I left Richard's car and ran to the train just as it was leaving the station. The long cars of the Chicago and Northwestern Railway had doors in the middle with a small platform to step up to the doors. But before I could get inside the train, the doors closed.

After I jumped on the tiny step with my left hand gripping the side of the train and my right hand holding my attaché case, the train started moving faster than usual. So fast, I was afraid to jump back to the ground. I assumed the conductor in that car would see me and open the doors.

There were three major problems with my assumption. First, the train I jumped on was an express train, gathering speed much faster than the local ones I normally rode. The second problem was because it was an express train, conductors took tickets only at a few major stops after leaving downtown Chicago and there was only one conductor for every three or four cars. My car had none. The third problem was the express train did not stop at Highwood and it was going too fast to jump to the elevated tracks below the train.

The faces of passengers standing in the middle of the car revealed some of them must have realized what I had just remembered, causing fear to pulse through my body. They probably also knew about the sign I saw every day on a bridge separating Highwood and Lake Forest. The sign boldly proclaimed, "Car will not clear man on side of car."

Perhaps you have heard that just before approaching death, your whole life passes through your mind. That hap-

Chapter Five: What I Discovered in Graduate School

Was it just another day in the life of a graduate student? Was it a miracle? Or was Someone on that train step with me?

pened to me that day. In nanoseconds, my birth, farm days, and school days flashed through my mind. I knew that sign was true on the approaching bridge that it would not clear a man on the side of the car. My only thought was, "Should I jump now or try to get so close to the train it would not knock me off?"

I chose the latter. Somehow, the extra pounds of my body compressed into my stomach and I flattened like a pancake against the side of the train, desperately also holding my attaché case flat against the train. My ungloved hands were nearly frozen to the train from both fear and the temperature.

The bridge hit my bottom, almost whisking me away with it. But after we passed the bridge, miraculously perhaps, I was still standing on the tiny step by the doors of the train. Someone found a conductor in another car, with the key needed to open the door and let me enter.

"That bridge will not clear a man on the side of the car," the conductor exclaimed. "I know," I replied. "But it did!" The conductor was so shaken by the experience, he fell, and passengers helped him to a seat.

I found a vacant seat also, one with a newspaper on it, and read the newspaper until we reached Lake Forest. I got off the train and waited for the next local to Lake Bluff. Was it just another day in the life of a graduate student? Was it a miracle? Or was Someone on that train step with me?

Bayesian Statistics

If you are above a certain age, you might remember seeing the classic TV police program *Dragnet*. If you are below a certain age, you might still see episodes on stations featuring reruns of classics. In either case, you will see Sgt. Joe Friday interviewing witnesses expressing opinions about details of a crime. Sgt. Friday always confronted their opinions and is attributed to saying the phrase "Just the facts, ma'am. Just the facts."

Collecting facts and separating fact from fiction, experience, or opinion is the essence of most doctoral programs. Whether the subject is physics, psychology, or chemical engineering, the standard for establishing truth is based on research methodology to gather evidence. I wish all people could take courses that teach how to separate fact from fake.

My first year at Northwestern placed me in classes with world experts on research methodology: professors like Dr. Ben Underwood, who wrote the classic textbook *Experimental Psychology*; one of my favorite courses was Cross Cultural Research taught by Dr. Donald Campbell, the world's best known expert on experimental and quasi-experimental research in the social sciences; and a Ph.D. seminar attracting students from every discipline on campus, taught by Dr. Scott Greer using his book *The Logic of Social Inquiry*. Dr. Phil Kotler taught my course on quantitative modeling. Phil also became a friend for life, before, during and after prison. These and other courses imbued me with a philosophy of evidence-based decisions, whether the question involves medicine, physics, economics, or philosophy.

The research course that had eternal impact on me, however, was a quantitative methods course using the textbook *Probability and Statistics for Business Decisions* by Robert Schlai-

Chapter Five: What I Discovered in Graduate School

fer, a pioneer in Bayesian decision theory at the Harvard Business School. Professor Schlaifer referred to the work of an 18th-century English mathematician, Thomas Bayes, who first used probability inductively and established a mathematical basis for probability inference. Today, Bayesian theory is used for a wide range of marketing decisions and practical problems such as forecasting weather, identifying email spam, and identifying forgeries. It is central to the latest developments in artificial intelligence.

How do you calculate the probability of something that has never happened before, such as marketers must do with the introduction of a new product? Traditional statistics does not have an answer for that, but Bayesian statisticians combine the probability of things that are known to calculate probability of the unknown.

The most important application of Bayesian statistics, it seemed to me, was the applications friends and students of Bayes, who was also a minister, made concerning the existence of God.

The most important application of Bayesian statistics, it seemed to me, was the applications friends and students of Bayes, who was also a minister, made concerning the existence of God. Did the Earth, humans, the tides that rejuvenate the oceans and create weather that makes life possible on Earth, and the complexity of the human eye just happen by chance, or were they designed by a Creator? What caused the galaxies, our planet, and human life? "If you don't know the cause, you won't know the cure" was the phrase I used to begin a previous book, *Saving America*, which describes how to start and grow a business.

As it turns out, people who calculate the probability of the Earth and life being caused by chance instead of a Creator face huge odds of being wrong. In most scholarly research, variables that have a probability of less than .05 level of significance can be attributed to an independent cause. With calculations of all the operations of Earth being caused by chance, the probability is .00000000000000000001 or less, enough to get accepted in any research journal. This was much different than the conclusion of my history professor when I was an undergraduate.

The existence or nonexistence of God was also a major question investigated by Blaise Pascal, French mathematician, physicist, and religious philosopher. He posits that humans bet with their lives that God either exists or does not, arguing that living as though God exists and seeking to believe in God is a much better wager than betting your life there is no God—and being wrong.

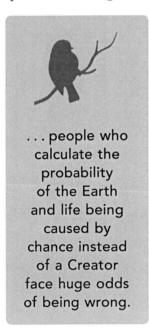

... people who calculate the probability of the Earth and life being caused by chance instead of a Creator face huge odds of being wrong.

While these statistical and probabilistic arguments are not without counterarguments, they caused me to consider the advantages of belief in God (or G-d for Jewish readers) compared to disbelief. Belief wins. This question caused me to dig deeper, reading books that examined the archaeological evidence concerning biblical teachings, the logic of comparative religions,

Chapter Five: What I Discovered in Graduate School

and whether scientific evidence conflicts or confirms biblical principles. Even prominent atheists such as Richard Dawkins and Christopher Hitchens are troubled by the "fine tuning" of the universe. They have no explanation for the fact that 122 variables need to be lined up with perfect precision for our universe to exist. If any of those go astray, just a little bit, it will all implode. And yet over all these years, it has been in perfect harmony and with great precision. ***It takes too much faith in the unexplainable and too much belief in existential nothingness to be an atheist.***

Atheism requires too much faith and too few facts to live life as an atheist.

A friend in Lake Bluff gave me the book *Mere Christianity*, by C. S. Lewis, the famous English author of such works as *The Chronicles of Narnia* and *The Screwtape Letters*. As a confirmed atheist at Cambridge University, C. S. Lewis debated Christian professors for years until one day he realized the logic of Christianity was correct and the non-logic of atheism was indefensible. And if God can create the world, He can certainly create human life. And if God can create human life, He is also capable of creating a method to communicate with His creation. It is called the Bible. A more recent book by Tim Keller, *The Reason for God*, is also very convincing with answers that an open-minded person has difficulty refuting. My faith in atheism was destroyed. Atheism requires too much faith and too few facts to live life as an atheist.

As C. S. Lewis states, at the end of life, the question that determines your eternity is whether a person says to God,

"Your will be done," or whether God says to that person, "Your will be done." I concluded that God caused life as we know it and asked Christ to be part of my life prior to studying Bayesian statistics. But after studying Bayesian statistics, I recognized my faith should rely not only on opinion but on facts—the kind of evidence Ph.D. students learn in research methodology courses.

By "chance," I met a brilliant marketing person named Henry Robertz, the president of a design firm that prepared marketing materials for such firms as McDonald's (including the famous arches that symbolize its stores) and Chicago Bridge and Iron. A talented fine artist as well as commercial designer, he accompanied me on my first trip to the Chicago Art Institute, where I developed an interest in contemporary art. Hank also invited me to a Bible study in his home taught by Dr. Millard Erickson, where I learned the value of studying the Bible in a small group.

That group contained people with exceptional intellectual skills focused on understanding the Bible. Several were students or faculty at nearby Trinity seminary, who read their Bibles in Greek. Doug was a professor at Trinity, educated in Israel, and an expert on Masoretic Text, the authoritative Hebrew Bible that Christians call the Old Testament. Friedhelm was a Ph.D. student at the University of Chicago completing his dissertation on the writings of Johann Wolfgang von Goethe. He was also an instructor in German at Lake Forest College and studied from his Luther translation of the Bible. Isaac Wong, librarian at Lake Forest College, read from his Chinese New Testament. We spent an entire year analyzing the book of James and its meaning in everyday life, sometimes dissecting a single verse for hours with the advantage of these rich backgrounds to understand not only English translations of the verses but their meaning in

Chapter Five: What I Discovered in Graduate School

the culture in which they were written, a field of study called Hermeneutics. That is where I learned the power of small group study of the Bible and the ability of God to provide His creation with a reliable authority on His nature and plans for the lives of His creation.

Dr. Erickson, our leader with the Ph.D. from Northwestern, also had a degree from Chicago University in Existential Philosophy and was preparing a manuscript on Christian Systematic Theology. He asked me, as a layperson with limited knowledge of the Bible, to read his manuscript for suggestions on how to communicate essential concepts of Biblical Christianity. As I read his book (which later became a standard text in universities), I found answers to the often trivial controversies that keep people from understanding the eternal truths contained in the Bible. Among other lessons, I learned it is prudent to base doctrines on a holistic understanding of Bible themes rather than a single verse.

Through good times and some bad times in my life, I discovered that God goes with people who love Him through both the good and the bad, even in prison, just like He did with Moses in the Red Sea and 40 years getting to the Promised Land. But only for those who seek a relationship with God. God invites us to know Him personally but does not force His will on people who believe they can live life by themselves and fail to invite Him into their lives. I came to

God goes with people who love Him through both the good and the bad, ...just like He did with Moses in the Red Sea and 40 years getting to the Promised Land. But only for those who seek a relationship with God.

realize that when I was clutching to the door handle of that train: I was not alone.

Maybe I would have encountered the same experience at Harvard or Wharton as I did at Northwestern, but probably not. ***I hope you now understand why Bayesian statistics was a catalyst for the most eternally valuable discovery I made as a graduate student at Northwestern.***

CHAPTER SIX

Dusty and a Guardian Angel

THE SUCCESS of professors at major research universities is determined heavily by the quantity and quality of research that can be published with significant results. "Significant" has a specific meaning in scholarly journals. Significant usually means less than 5% ($p = .05$) chance the observed effects occurred by chance or random assignment. When it is especially important to avoid a false conclusion about cause and effect, sometimes the level of significance is raised to 1% or $p = .01$.

Because of the need to run a lot of experiments to publish such results, professors may spend a lot of their time in a laboratory but normally publish only the "significant" results. When an event occurs with a low probability of an alternative plausible hypothesis, conclusions are made about what caused the observed results.

Some events occur in everyday life with a low probability of occurring by chance. If the probability of that event occurring by chance is extremely low, it is sometimes called a "miracle" in the laboratory of life.

What you are about to read below is exactly as my father described it. Rather than relate the narrative secondhand, I will reprint verbatim Dad's words from his book *Farm Boy*. Please make your own conclusion whether the event happened "by chance" or "by miracle."

Dusty by Dale Blackwell

Dusty was a small Shetland pony purchased for my grandson, Christian, to ride when he came to Missouri to stay with us for a month when he was four years old. When Christian came, he and Dusty bonded almost immediately. He soon found that he could take a light rope out into the pasture, walk up to Dusty, place the rope around her neck, and lead her up to the barn. But Dusty wanted nothing to do with me. She wouldn't let me get close to her. When I wanted to catch her, I had to drive her up into the barn lot with a few of the cattle she was with.

Later in the winter, she was part of a miracle that saved my life. We had a 16-inch snowfall—deepest of the winter. I waited at home until the snowplows cleared the highway down to the farm only a mile-and-a-half away. I left the pickup at the outside gate and walked through the deep snow to the hay barn one-fourth mile down a lane and into the pasture. I threw out 75 bales and had dragged away about half when a terrific pain hit my left chest and into the left shoulder and arm.

I dropped to a bale of hay but remained conscious. The pain was so sudden and severe, I felt sure it was a heart attack, and I would not survive. But I felt something rubbing the top of my right shoulder. I looked up and there was Dusty!

I doubted it could be possible but decided to try to get on her. She stood perfectly still, and I made it. With my heavy high-top

Chapter Six: Dusty and a Guardian Angel

Dr. Dale J. Blackwell, grandson Christian Blackwell, and Dusty

overshoes dragging in the deep snow, she started walking to the lane and toward the pickup.

At about every one-hundred yards she would stop, and I feared she wanted me to get off. Then she would walk on about another hundred yards until she walked around the barn and right up to the gate where the pickup was. When I got off, she turned around and started running back toward where the cows were eating their hay. My chest pain was gone. I walked through the gate, got into the pickup, and drove home.

What does this occurrence and similar rescues and protection, including our son Roger's miracle restoration to life after being treated as a stillborn baby, indicate to me? Did Dusty know a pickup was available to me one-quarter mile away? Did Dusty know I was too weak to walk through the deep snow to the pickup? Did Dusty know to walk there without the aid of a bridle or halter? Did Dusty decide on her own to be a friend and helper?

To me, the answers are obvious and explainable. I believe one or more guardian angels were guiding Dusty to protect my life. I believe in angels.

CHAPTER SEVEN

Go Bucks!

RETURNING TO Missouri was my plan, probably teaching in one of many good state universities, maybe even Northwest State or Mizzou. Chicago, however, was an exciting place to live with its diversity of entertainment, restaurants, and museums. And we had good friends in Lake Bluff and Lake Forest. I would have been delighted to remain as a professor at Northwestern, but remaining where you receive your Ph.D. is rare in academics. And there were others in the Northwestern Ph.D. program who would have been better qualified than me to remain where they received their Ph.D.

Another university in Chicago offered a position, but when I told my advisor about it, he said, "Roger, you can go any place you choose, but we did not invest resources of the faculty and the scholarship money in you to go to any school that is not a major research university." He was right, and I went "on the market" at the annual meeting of the American Marketing Association. The AMA meeting that year was in Chicago, which allowed me to interview with many schools at low cost and receive several offers, including three Big 10 schools. All three had excellent faculties and research opportunities.

My dissertation had co-advisors, something cautious doctoral students probably would not do. One advisor was from the Economics Department at NU, and the other from the Kellogg School of Management. This was important because my topic was a quantitative and cross-cultural analysis of the effects of entry regulation on price levels in a differentiated oligopoly. The research data base was from the funeral industry, chosen because data are more complete and publicly available than in other industries. One of the Northwestern professors who would have been a logical advisor refused to serve on a dissertation about death, probably because it reminded him of his own mortality. Two of the Big 10 universities made offers but wanted me to refrain from talking about death. All three universities offered the same salary—$9,600 a year.

During my campus visit to Ohio State, the faculty not only asked meaningful questions about my death research but arranged a lunch with executives of the Ohio Funeral Directors Association who offered support continuing my research in this area if I accepted the Ohio State position. Also, Jim Engel and Alton Doody, professors of marketing at Ohio State, took me to a "candlelight close" dinner ending with the assertion, "If you live in the cities of the other universities you are considering, you will only have opportunities provided by the university. If you live in Columbus, Ohio, your biggest challenge will be choosing from the many opportunities in Columbus as well as Ohio State."

The decision of which offer to accept was obvious. At age 25, I became an Assistant Professor of Marketing at The Ohio State University. Go, Bucks!

Chapter Seven: Go Bucks!

Professor James Engel

One of the best known professors in the newly emerging field of consumer behavior was Dr. James Engel, an authority on motivation research and a major reason David Kollat, from Indiana University, and I chose OSU the same year to become Assistant Professors. Soon after Dave and I arrived, Jim invited us to join him in teaching a seminar for his remarkable Ph.D. students.

That seminar resulted in a trilogy of books. *Consumer Behavior* was published by the three of us in 1967, providing a pioneering conceptual model for teaching consumer behavior that became known as the Engel, Kollat, Blackwell (EKB) model of consumer decision-making. Over the next 40 years that text sold over a million copies in 10 editions and a dozen languages. The rest of the trilogy included Cases in *Consumer Behavior* and *Research in Consumer Behavior.* Those books and the articles we jointly authored in scholarly journals established Ohio State as a premier institution to study consumer behavior.

A workshop that Jim convened for the American Marketing Association in Columbus created a new organization, called the Association for Consumer Research. Today, ACR includes 1,700 researchers from all over the world. I recently attended the 50th anniversary of ACR in Atlanta, wishing Jim could have been there to see the role he played in creating a global research community.

One of my first days at Ohio State, I was standing in my office (because the chair that had been ordered weeks earlier had not yet arrived) when Jim came bouncing into the office Dave and I shared. Jim was a high-energy person! I did not know it until then, but Jim had become a Christian since the time of my initial interview, thanks to the ministry of Campus Crusade for Christ (now known as CRU). After welcoming me, some of his first words were "I heard from a friend in Chicago that you are a Christian. Is that true?"

"Yes," I answered.

"I mean truly a Christian with the Holy Spirit in your life?" Jim continued.

"Yes," I again responded, and we formed a friendship lasting eternally.

Jim was president of the Christian Faculty Fellowship at Ohio State, which held breakfast meetings attracting hundreds of faculty members from every department of the university. Speakers included such people as opera singer Jerome Hines, but the biggest attraction was Billy Graham, who spoke to the faculty one morning while conducting a Crusade in Columbus. I still sometimes repeat one of the jokes Billy told at that breakfast about a man who entered an airplane somewhat inebriated and talking loudly. He sat in the row in front of Graham without recognizing him. When the flight attendant came to his seat and asked him to be quieter, noting Billy Graham was in the seat behind his, the man got up out of his seat, put out his hand, and said to Billy Graham, "You shore have helped me." I always remembered that story and sometimes mentioned it when someone said something good about how my speech helped them.

Jim also became the National Faculty Director for Campus Crusade and organized a workshop on evangelism at the Conrad Hilton Hotel in Chicago for prominent professors from the U.S. and Canada. The workshop was taught by Dr. Bill Bright, and I was fortunate enough to attend along with scholars from many campuses. By that time in my life, I had studied the intellectual reasons for belief but had never studied how to help nonbelievers in their decision to accept

Jesus Christ as their Savior. That seminar was life-changing for me. It was exciting to observe professors explaining to interested people "The Four Spiritual Laws," a basic outline explaining how to invite Jesus into their life.

Billy Graham eventually was the reason Jim left our team at Ohio State to become the Billy Graham Professor of Communications at Wheaton College in Chicago, where he wrote a major book on evangelism called *Contemporary Christian Communications, Its Theory and Practice,* which contains the "Engel Scale" showing how people progress from interest in Christian faith to conversion. When Wheaton dedicated the Billy Graham Center and Library, Jim invited me to the ceremony. I sat at the luncheon table and talked with Billy Graham, the only person I respect as much or more than my own father.

Marketing 650

The basic marketing course at Ohio State for decades carried the title of Marketing 650, Principles of Marketing. In my early years at Ohio State, it was taught by two master teachers, Dr. William Davidson and Dr. Alton Doody, who had developed effective techniques for teaching that engaged hundreds of students in an auditorium and employed graduate assistants to administer the testing process.

The first few years at Ohio State I taught undergraduate classes in consumer behavior and marketing research and MBA courses in quantitative analysis and strategy. I also taught a large class on Death and Dying, enrolling students from throughout the campus with large numbers from nursing and medical school. For reasons I will not take your time to detail, I also taught courses in Black Marketing as a (only white) member of the Black Studies Faculty. These were courses where I got to know well most of the students, both in and after class, and I wondered how that could be done with classes as large as Marketing 650.

Dr. Davidson and Dr. Doody left Ohio State to start Management Horizons, which became the leading retail consulting firm in the world. When the topic of who would replace Davidson and Doody in Marketing 650 was discussed in a faculty meeting, most of the fingers pointed at me.

Marketing 650 was originally taught in Hagerty 100, which held about 300 students. The demand increased so much that the university moved the afternoon section to Independence Hall, a building with one classroom of 750 seats. The room was usually filled, often with a waiting list of 50-60 or more. The evening section of Marketing 650 remained in Hagerty 100, making me responsible for about 1,000 students per quarter. Usually, I taught those sections two quarters a year, but some years three quarters plus a course (with many fewer students) of Consumer Behavior or an Honors section of Marketing 650. It was both draining and rewarding to teach 2,000 to 3,000 students or more each year.

One of the papers I presented at the American Marketing Association was "Managing Marketing Mega Sections," describing how to engage 750 students and grade them more carefully than a single professor can do in a normal-size class. Although it was my job to engage every student in a room of 750, the key to the whole process was my staff of student assistants. Students who received an A for the course received a personal letter serving as an employment reference but also asking if they would like to become a grader next term. The pay was reasonably good for a campus job, but also provided personal interaction when we met before the grading of each case, usually four papers per term by each student. I knew the A students understood what constituted an excellent paper because that is what they had written before the invitation to become a grader. Our grading assistants took off one point for every spelling and grammar error, and graders were expected to add written comments on each page of the papers they graded describing how to improve both content and writing. People are sometimes surprised to learn that grading is more comprehensive, objective, and helpful with a process such as this than in small classes where the instructor often writes, "B, needs improvement."

Some students do better on multiple-choice exams, and some do better with essays, so every student was given their choice of which to take. Thankfully, most chose multiple-choice exams because I graded the essay exams myself. Students could submit a written appeal on any case or exam they believed unfairly graded, but few did.

The process was effective not only because of the A students who graded written cases but also because the truly exceptional graders were offered a position with a full-ride scholarship and stipend to enter the MBA program as Teaching Assistants. They managed the grading process but also staffed office hours so that students had access to help every day of the week including some evening office hours, as well as triaged problems to me. There were usually two TAs each year, allowing me to get to know some exceptional people. Many remained good friends after leaving the MBA or Ph.D. program, and several of the doctoral students won teaching awards when they became faculty members at other universities. Those TAs and the student graders allowed Marketing 650 at Ohio State to provide more personal help to students than courses that have only one instructor and limited office hours and grading.

We were fortunate to participate in a standardized testing program with marketing classes in 80 universities. Most of those schools had smaller classes and higher admission qualifications than Ohio State, but the OSU marketing mega courses always performed in the top quintile and usually the top decile of performance in the nation.

Published research papers in education journals report greater learning in large classes than small sections, which surprises some people. The reason for those findings is that the determinant of learning is the quality of teaching, not the size of the class. Large classes and properly managed staff achieve better learning than small classes by poorly paid teachers and inadequate grading. When we used this process at Ohio State, we achieved superior learning at about a fifth of the cost of small classes while also providing financial assistance to student graders and graduate assistants.

My passion was to engage students not only with *marketing principles* but also with *life skills*. I have been blessed to receive messages by letter, email, and greetings in person relating the value they received in Marketing 650 from many of the 65,000 students in my 40 years of teaching at Ohio State. Many of those students remain close friends today, some among my closest friends. They say I had a major effect on their life, but nothing compared to the effect those 65,000 students have had on mine.

In addition to the 65,000 students in the Marketing 650 class and other courses at Ohio State, there were hundreds more students when I was a Visiting Professor at Stanford, the University of Washington, Guelph (in Canada), and multiple years teaching in African universities plus thousands more in executive education programs on six continents. Because of longevity and the size of my classes, I believe I had more students than any professor at Ohio State. Since OSU is one of the largest universities in the nation, it may be true that I taught more students than any professor in the U.S., although

Chapter Seven: Go Bucks!

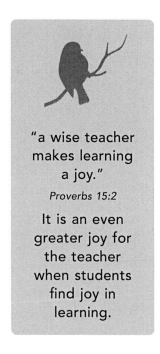

"a wise teacher makes learning a joy."
Proverbs 15:2

It is an even greater joy for the teacher when students find joy in learning.

I cannot verify that extrapolation. There is a Proverb (15:2) saying, "a wise teacher makes learning a joy." It is an even greater joy for the teacher when students find joy in learning.

Over the years, there were offers to be a chaired professor or dean at other universities, but I always declined for two reasons. First, I became increasingly aware of the plan God had for me, and it was teaching, not being an administrator. Second, though I enjoyed the world-class students I taught at Stanford and Northwestern, my greatest joy was teaching students at Ohio State who came from every spectrum of society. Many were the first in their family to graduate from college.

If I were ever to return to a university in the future, my best contribution would probably be teaching other teachers how to engage, motivate, and improve learning with methods that achieve higher productivity and lower costs, a great need in today's schools. Those were lessons I learned from teaching Marketing 650 along with the joy I received from the messages of thousands of students after 40 years teaching at Ohio State.

Many of the messages from former students begin or end saying Marketing 650 changed their life—sometimes economically, sometimes personally, and sometimes spiritually. Some of those students remain today among my closest friends. They often express thanks for what they learned in my classes, but I am even more thankful for what I learned from them. One of the blessings of being a teacher is the opportunity to see tomorrow before it happens.

Boards

In addition to teaching a lot of students, leading executive seminars, and writing books, I have been asked to serve on corporate boards—too many, as you will see in the next chapter. Serving on corporate boards is much like having a child. Sometimes you must do little except watch the child achieve good grades, sports awards, and graduation honors. Sometimes, however, serving on a corporate board is like being the parent of a troubled teenager.

Some of the boards that were the most fun were start-ups in which I also invested funds along with sweat equity. One of those turned a $28,000 investment into enough value when it became public to pay for my new home. Another public board grew from a small investment into enough shares to donate the salary of my entire career back to Ohio State before I retired. In return, Ohio State named a building the Roger Blackwell Executive Residence (aka the Blackwell Inn) at the Max Fisher School of Business.

The greatest rewards, however, are messages from former students referencing what they learned in classes. Some also comment about something I said or distributed in class that helped in their own journey toward Christian faith and a personal relationship with our Creator. In later years, I put into writing my philosophy of life and made it available on the last day of class to students who wanted a copy. Just before the final chapter of this book, you will find what I wrote and offered to students, described as *Roger's Rules for a Successful Life*.

Chapter Seven: Go Bucks!

If God told us His total plan for our entire life, we might say "no thanks." But that is not the way He does it. God reveals His plan step by step, allowing us the choice to say yes or no.

The journey I took through life was not the one I planned nor would have dreamed possible. If God told us His total plan for our entire life, we might say "no thanks." But that is not the way He does it. God reveals His plan step by step, allowing us the choice to say yes or no. Some never learn His plan because they never say yes along the way. In Jeremiah 29:11, I learned that Someone else had a plan for my life, one that prospered me, and despite the events described in the next chapter, gave me hope for the future. As C.S. Lewis once wrote, ***"You can't go back and change your beginning, but you can start where you are and change the ending."***

CHAPTER EIGHT

FCI Morgantown

HAVE YOU ever thought about how likely you are to be sent to prison for six years? What would you have to do for that to happen to you?

As I rode silently on the passenger side of my car through the rolling Appalachian hills on a cold, rainy January morning in 2006, I thought silently how I might have answered those same questions in the past.

You could have asked about most any dire consequence that could happen, and I would have considered it more likely than going to prison. Death in my family? A major medical problem for myself? Those would have been likely for a person my age. Maybe even a financial reversal or a forced retirement. But, never in a thousand years would I have considered any possibility of going to prison.

From the first board I joined at age 29 and throughout the 13 other public boards I served on, lawyers cautioned directors and officers not to disclose confidential material information to anyone who was not a director or officer. When

Chapter Eight: FCI Morgantown

people ask questions about information not yet public, lawyers tell directors to respond, "I can't comment."

People in 1999 did ask about Worthington Foods (WFDS), a health food company on whose board I served. You may remember that 1999 was the zenith of the dot.com era, when tech stocks were soaring and brick-and-mortar stocks were stagnant. WFDS stock was not widely held, and many of the shareholders were friends or family of WFDS employees and officers because of Worthington's Seventh Day Adventist background manufacturing plant-based meat analogues. When the stock dropped from 20 that summer to 13, many WFDS stockholders bought more shares. They knew the company had a long history of good dividends and growth in the production and marketing of plant-based meat substitutes (like later products such as Beyond Meat and Impossible Burgers). In the summer of 1999 Worthington executives were approached by Kellogg, which was interested in adding vegetarian products. Kellogg became more interested when Worthington missed an earnings estimate and the stock price plummeted.

While the stock was dropping, over 6,000 people bought WFDS stock, many with close relationships to WFDS directors and employees. One of those purchasers was my office manager. She and her husband had been buying WFDS for years, attended annual shareholder meetings, and thought highly enough of WFDS that it was the largest holding in their IRA. When the stock dropped to 13, they added to their already substantial shares and continued buying until the price dropped below 11. My assistant asked me once why there were additional board meetings, and I answered as attorneys had instructed: "I can't comment on any of my board meetings." My son, my father, and others also asked about the falling price of WFDS stock. A few years later, under oath, they testified my response was always "I can't comment on any of the companies on whose board I serve."

There were no other conversations with my assistant about Worthington Foods, but like many others, she and her husband added to their holdings understanding the current price of WFDS was lower than its value. Kellogg also recognized WFDS stock was lower than its value, one of the reasons Kellogg was trying to acquire Worthington. When the sale did occur on October 1, people received $24 per share. I did not buy any stock myself or benefit from anyone who did, but the SEC began investigating me, possibly because I gave speeches recommending annual reporting of financial data by public corporations instead of quarterly. Warren Buffet also recommended the change for the same reason I advocated it: to promote long-range strategy instead of "short-term thinking" and the shenanigans that sometimes occur around quarterly earnings reports. Annual reporting, however, would reduce dramatically the number of employees needed at the SEC.

My attorneys reported the SEC was willing to settle the case for an amount less than the amount I had in my checking account. My response was, "If you are innocent, why would you pay the government anything?" I soon learned why.

The Department of Justice says it wins over 90% of criminal cases, and some studies indicate the number is higher, about 96%. If you go to trial and lose, which is almost always, the sentence is 3 to 5 times longer. That is why 97% of people who are accused of a crime take a plea even when they are innocent. If I agreed to a plea, I would not have to admit or deny guilt, would not have risked a felony conviction, and would not have lost the career I dearly loved at Ohio State. I should have written the check for the substan-

Chapter Eight: FCI Morgantown

tial but manageable fine, but I did not. There's a country song with lyrics saying, "I fought the law and the law won." I now understand that song.

The attorneys charged $9.1 million for the trial, another law firm charged $2.7 million for the appeal, and I was fined $1,000,000 plus accrued interest. I did not buy stock and did not benefit in any way from the 6,000 people who did. There was no evidence of any kind that I disclosed confidential information to my office manager or her husband, but they received sentences of 27 months and 24 months because they added to their holdings of WFDS even though they received no information from me.

My attorneys were confident I would be found not guilty. What they did not know was how the case was switched from the original judge to one with whom I had a prior association. When I was not present, that judge, recorded by the court reporter, said, "Like many in the community, I know Mr. Blackwell. In fact, when I was in private practice, he was an expert witness for me."

The truth was I was an expert witness against him, but if he had said that he would have had to recuse himself. A court document that proved I was an expert against him before he became a Federal Judge mysteriously "disappeared" from the courthouse in Columbus. An attorney investigator I later hired found a copy of the original document in the basement of a storage facility in Chicago showing I was a witness against the judge when he was in private practice. The copy submitted by the judge in his answer was identical to the one the investigator discovered in Chicago, except the copy the judge filed was missing the essential document about my testimony. The other professor who worked with me on the case also submitted a notarized affidavit of our work against his case while the judge was in private practice. I could not obtain those documents until after I was in prison, and then it was too late because recusal must be requested before a trial, the appeal court ruled.

There was another fact I did not know until after the trial. My former wife called me and said, "How could he be the judge in your case when he was the one who encouraged me to file a divorce against you and obtained a divorce attorney for me?" She also signed a notarized affidavit explaining the activities of the judge in our divorce. That was also after I was in prison, so the issue was ruled "moot" when I asked for a retrial.

During the trial, my attorneys hired expert witnesses, including Professor Jarrell, a former SEC Chief Economist. After reviewing NASDAQ records, he discovered that nearly all the Worthington directors had numerous friends and family who bought WFDS stock during the time period discussions were occurring with Kellogg, probably for the same reasons my assistant and her husband bought stock. Some of the directors had twice as many associates as I did buy stock when the price dropped, and the Jarrell chart showed the names of all of them. When the judge saw the chart in a sidebar, his face turned red and he refused to let the expert testify about the chart. Although the judge refused to let that expert testify, my attorney briefly flashed it on the screen during closing arguments. During jury deliberation, the jury sent a note asking the judge to see only one thing—the Jarrell Chart. The judge refused to let the jury see it. I believe he knew if the jury saw the chart, it would have resulted in my being found not guilty.

I have written another manuscript describing the details of what happened in my case, but it has not been published for two reasons. First, there probably would not be many people interested in reading it. Second, in addition to a fine

Chapter Eight: FCI Morgantown

of a million dollars and a prison sentence of six years, the judge added an unusual condition to my sentence. "The defendant shall not profit in any way from the production of books, movies, or any other media products that may occur as a result of his involvement in the instant offense."

I believe the judge would have tried to send me back to prison if I published that manuscript, titled *Conviction at any Cost*, so if it is ever published, it will be posthumously. I am confident if the judge sends federal marshals to retrieve me from Heaven, St. Peter will not allow them through the pearly gates!

During my time in prison, I was able to make copies of *Roger's Rules for a Successful Life*, which I previously distributed to thousands of students in college and executive classes and now distributed to fellow inmates (and even a few corrections officers!). Those rules are included at the end of the next chapter. People have asked what I would do if I were in a room today and the judge entered. My answer is I would go back and reread Rules #1 and #2. Especially Rule #2.

A machine gun full of memories occupied my thoughts as my son delivered me to prison, many of them about events you've read in this book. Life as a university professor had been good, the fulfillment of what I knew for decades was my calling—teaching. That rainy January morning, I spent time thinking about the many years I lived my life in an academic environment, far different I knew, from the future years now facing me.

I also thought about the role my faith played throughout four decades of diverse, demanding, but rewarding activities. I wondered how that faith would be tested in prison. Those were the thoughts racing through my mind as my son drove from Columbus for "self-surrender," a much-preferred alternative, I soon learned, to "diesel therapy," the entry to prison for many. My self-surrender was to the Federal Correctional Institution (FCI) in Morgantown, West Virginia.

Get a Job!

If you have an image of prison as a place where people sleep and read all day in a prison cell, think again. Everyone must have a job. Whether it is cleaning facilities, cooking food, mowing lawns, doing laundry, washing and driving cars for the warden, or making things the prison sells to generate revenue, everyone must work. If water pipes freeze on a cold winter night, the guards wake up the inmate with the job of emergency plumber. The work of prison staff is to carry keys and conduct head counts.

On my first day, after receiving a prison uniform and steel-toed work shoes, I was ordered where every inmate begins—Administration and Orientation (A&O), a two-week period where everyone learns the rules they must obey for survival. After that, inmates are assigned a job, initially something such as "A.M. Food Service." Getting up at 4:30 in the morning to cook, wash dishes, and scrub floors was my probable assignment for the first few years of prison.

On my second day, while I was starting A&O, an inmate brought a note to me from the Literacy Director ordering me to report to her in the Education Building. I left A&O and reported to Ms. Hayes.

When I met her, she said, "Some of the inmates say you write books; is that true?" I responded affirmatively. Then she added, "We have difficulty finding inmates to teach the grammar parts of our GED courses. Do you think you could do that?"

"I've never taught grammar," I responded, "but I am willing to try." Instead of A&O, she told me to report to the

Chapter Eight: FCI Morgantown

Education Building at 7:30 a.m. the next day and she would observe me teaching a grammar course. She did not know about my background as a teacher, and she probably did not know I prepared that night as much for that GED class as I would for an MBA class. I got the job and started the following day, teaching not only grammar but literature, science, math, and government—the five areas that must be passed to receive a GED. What she did not know, nor did I until a couple of weeks later, was what happened one hour before she sent the message to meet in her office.

Prior to prison, I was a member of a Bible study group of men meeting in Upper Arlington Lutheran Church. We met every Tuesday morning at 6:45 and rotated teaching among ourselves. On the second day of my incarceration, back in Columbus, the men in my Bible study took the normal hour of study to pray that my skills as a teacher would be used while I was in prison. One hour later, unknown to them, Ms. Hayes sent the note ordering me to her office to talk about teaching grammar. Was the timing just a coincidence? Or was it another Miracle, the kind of intervention God sometimes makes in the lives of His followers when he promises them "You are not alone"?

... the men in my Bible study took the normal hour of study to pray that my skills as a teacher would be used while I was in prison.... One hour later, Ms. Hayes sent the note ordering me to her office to talk about teaching grammar. Was the timing just a coincidence? Or was it another Miracle, the kind of intervention God sometimes makes in the lives of His followers when he promises them "You are not alone"?

Graduation Day

For five and a half years, I taught GED courses to men who did not graduate from high school, most with very different backgrounds than mine. About 60 percent were African-Americans, 20 percent Latinos, and 10 percent older white men (who previously sold meth or "White Lightning" in the West Virginia, Kentucky, and Tennessee mountains). I taught them English, literature, math, science, and government, and they taught me about survival in the hood and mountains.

Teaching in prison is by inmates called "tutors." The staff are called "instructors," but their role is to carry keys and take attendance. Most of the tutors had a Ph.D., M.D., J.D. or some other professional degree. They were selected from 200 or so white-collar inmates in a prison holding 1,400 men, mostly there for drug and related crimes. When I taught classes on government, I sometimes invited two other inmates who had unique knowledge because of their former profession as U.S. Congressmen, one a Democrat and one a Republican. Some of the science classes were taught by the 30 or 40 physicians and dentists who were inmates at FCI Morgantown, usually there for tax cases.

After my first month of teaching, I received a paycheck of $25, which advanced to $50 a month by the end of my sentence. When I told my son, who is a public school teacher, he was excited and said, "Dad, this is the first time as a teacher, I am making more than you."

One day, Ms. Hayes noticed I spoke a little Spanish to some of the Latino students and asked if I could teach one section each day in Spanish because inmates are permitted to take the GED exam in Spanish. I was not fluent enough to do that but took two Spanish classes taught by Hispanic

Chapter Eight: FCI Morgantown

inmates, giving me enough fluency to teach a section in Spanish. One of my friends from outside sent brochures called "May I Share" in Spanish, explaining how to accept Christ, and everyone in the class in the next few months asked Jesus to be their Savior. They wanted to have a Fiesta to celebrate, but food and beverages were prohibited in the classroom. When I asked the instructor to make an exception, she did and one Friday afternoon, the Latino students prepared tacos in the microwaves of a housing unit. We purchased colas from commissary and had a Fiesta to celebrate the acceptance of Christ as their Savior.

During the almost six years I spent teaching in prison, several hundred men received their GEDs. Once a year, the prison held a graduation ceremony in the Visitors' Room, with diplomas, graduation caps and gowns, and all the pomp and circumstance of graduation outside prison. Inmates could invite two family members. One mother of an inmate in prison for transporting fireworks across the state line told me her two daughters both had Ph.D.s, but her son was never interested in school. She said, "I don't know how you got him interested in studying, but I am so thankful you did."

One of the graduates was about 6'8" and of enormous proportions. After he received his diploma, he picked me up about a foot off the ground, hugged me and said, "Thank you, man. I couldn't have done it without you." In addition to what I learned from 65,000 students at Ohio State, I learned lots more things from the several hundred students in my GED classes at FCI Morgantown, ranging from secrets of success selling drugs to how to survive as a Mafia hit man.

Over the years at Ohio State, I watched thousands of students graduate and placed a coveted Ph.D. hood over the gowns of some of them. It was just as rewarding to me to see men who mostly had graduated from serious crimes in the hood also graduate with a GED and a chance for a better life when they leave prison. ***A society that helps people in prison helps society have better people outside prison.***

CHAPTER NINE
Beyond Y2K

IT WAS almost six years after my son first drove me to FCI Morgantown, located at the base of a valley in the mountains of West Virginia. He returned to the same place in the same 1999 SUV and waited near R&D, a building that is both the worst and best place in prison. R stands for Receiving, making it a forbidding, traumatic place during admission. But D stands for Departures, and my son was waiting outside to help carry boxes of paper and books I accumulated in prison. R&D opens at 7 a.m. to receive and discharge inmates. On the November day of my departure, I did not leave as soon as it opened. I waited until 7:01.

There were several boxes, filled with books I read, handwritten books I wrote, hundreds of legal documents, and many journal pages reflecting nearly six years in prison. Camps are sometimes called "club feds" because they are less restrictive and house more white-collar inmates. FCI Morgantown was higher security than camps but lacked the controlled movements of high-security institutions. At FCI

Morgantown, nearly every moment is controlled, however, by standup counts and other restrictions—still a miserable place to spend six years.

Reading books interested me more than watching the one small TV tuned to programming tastes of 140 inmates in my housing unit. The books included classics by Dietrich Bonhoeffer such as *Cost of Discipleship and Life Together,* which I first read during my faith-formative days at Northwestern. I also read Bonhoeffer's *Letters from Prison* at Northwestern, but it took on new meaning with greater empathy when I reread it in prison. Bonhoeffer's *Prison* book shaped how I wrote letters and mailed copies to friends while in Morgantown. People who received those letters have suggested I should also publish them in a book called *Roger's Letters from Prison.* Maybe someday I will. An especially profound book I read was *Bonhoeffer: Pastor, Martyr, Prophet, Spy,* by Eric Metaxas, from which I made pages of notes and started a handwritten manuscript called *Prison Faith,* which someday I hope I can transform into a book to encourage others who want to know how faith survives in the miseries of prison.

The Language of God, by Francis Collins, was one of the best new books sent by friends, especially since the Spanish translation, *El lenguaje de Dios: Un Científico Presenta Evidencias Para Creer,* made a perfect gift for Latino friends who became Christians in my GED classes. Business friends also sent books on crowd sourcing, digital marketing, and other topics that I hoped would retain my marketing relevance as I looked toward the future. Books by people I worked with before prison such as Jack Welch, Michael Dell, Tom Peters, and Malcolm Gladwell encouraged me but sometimes brought tears to my eyes as I remembered better times in the past.

The boxes were also filled with documents sent via "legal mail" by my lawyers plus some I prepared *pro se* in the prison

Chapter Nine: Beyond Y2K

library. Jimmy, in the cell across from mine, was a Michigan Law graduate who represented celebrities on the outside but counselled me when I prepared a *writ of certiorari* to the U.S. Supreme Court, difficult to do *pro se* with only the resources of the prison's legal library. A clerk at the Supreme Court considered the *writ* sufficiently persuasive, and she wrote a detailed letter on how to conform to Supreme Court rules and contacted the Sixth Circuit, which claimed to have "lost" my appeal. The Circuit court "found" my appeal after her contact but dismissed the appeal without notifying me or allowing legal representation on the issue of asking for a different judge than the one who excluded evidence in my trial. You learn a lot about how the "justice" system works when you are in prison.

I spent five years sleeping on a steel plate called a "bed" covered with a one-inch cotton pad called a "mattress." I ate food daily that included some where inmates working in the kitchen had re-covered labels indicating it was several years beyond the expiration date. Those were the "good" meals because they were products fast-food chains disposed of by giving to prisons.

I observed inmates die for lack of medical care, including one of my GED students who fell from his upper bunk, hitting his head on the desk beside his bed. When the Prison Chaplain asked me to write a eulogy for him and a letter to his parents, I sent a copy to my pastor. When the message to my pastor was intercepted, the Medical Director tried to have me transferred to a high-security prison 1,000 miles from Columbus. After I argued my case before three lieutenants, they sent me outside the room while they deliberated. I could not hear exactly what they were saying but they were yelling at each other. I prayed, saying "God, I know you delivered three Jewish boys from a fiery furnace. Can you go into the room like that for me?" One of the lieutenants slammed the door as he left and said, "I voted to ship you." When the other two left the room, they smiled at me and said, "You are not being shipped." When they smiled and said I was not being shipped, I felt I had just escaped a fiery furnace—and was not in there alone!

Another lieutenant had a reputation so menacing that even the COs reporting to him tried to stay out of his way. When a new inmate mouthed off to him several times, other inmates warned the newbie to stay quiet, but he did not. The lieutenant took him to the SHU (Special Housing Unit), and other inmates heard the lieutenant beat the inmate to death. Fortunately, the inmate and the lieutenant were the same race. If it had been an interracial event, it could have caused a prison riot. The next morning, an official announcement said the inmate hung himself in the cell. Years later, when it was widely reported that Jeffrey Epstein committed suicide in a federal jail in New York, I understood how these things happen in prison.

In prison, there is always the risk of death or other trauma, especially when fights break out and guards come running from all directions. It was not unusual for guards to take the opportunity during a fight to beat prisoners they considered deserving of such treatment. The risk of sexual assault, I personally experienced, was greater from guards than from other inmates. You can understand why I so eagerly awaited my release from R&D.

I almost did not make it out. When I experienced an SVT (abnormally fast heart rhythm) after jogging on the track, I collapsed in the arms of Eric, whose cell was close to mine. Eric was an emergency physician before incarceration and took my pulse, alarmed it was over 240. He also knew the medical facility closed at 7 p.m., so he physically carried me

Chapter Nine: Beyond Y2K

 Was it just a coincidence that I collapsed in front of the only inmate who was formerly an emergency physician? Or was it, like my birth and exterior train ride, a miracle? I learned daily what God means when he promises "You are not alone."

to it just minutes before closing. About 100 yards from the door, he saw the nurse leaving, so he laid me on a bench and ran to the nurse, begging him to stay. When the nurse saw I was near death, he called the Morgantown EMS squad, and they took me to the University of West Virginia hospital, where I stayed a few days. I needed a pacemaker, but that was not something the prison wanted to do. It was delayed until my release, when it was installed at OSU Medical Center soon after I arrived home. Was it just a coincidence that I collapsed in front of the only inmate who was formerly an emergency physician? Or was it, like my birth and exterior train ride, a miracle? I learned daily what God means when he promises "You are not alone."

In the last few months and weeks of prison, every day seems to be 48 hours or longer and the nights seem to be holding back the break of day. In June, as I inched toward freedom that year, I was caught in a sudden thunderstorm with heavy, pelting rain. But almost as soon as it struck, it ended. I sat down on a well-used, rusting bench near the track where I had been jogging. To the east, I saw a vivid, double rainbow ending at the R&D building, disclosing again God's providential concern. To the west, I saw an intense sunset. The sun torched its brilliant rays up from the horizon to a long cloud stretching from north to south. The underside of the cloud glistened like pearls. It was then that

I understood that storm clouds do have a silver lining. I knew God had something better for me after leaving my time in the West Virginia valley.

Free at Last!

"Free at last, free at last, thank God Almighty, we are free at last." Those immortal words of Dr. Martin Luther King resonated in my mind on the way home from Morgantown. But unlike the prophetic words of Dr. King, neither he nor other people imprisoned by racial prejudice are truly free. Neither is someone leaving prison. I still faced three years of supervised release, or being "on paper" as it is often called.

The prison granted me, like most prisoners who avoid incident reports, the last six months in a halfway house in the city where I was sentenced. Therefore, my son could not take me home, where a good bed and good food would have welcomed me; he had to deliver me to Alvis House.

In many cities, a halfway house is the local jail, where conditions are often as criminal as some of the people housed there. Columbus is fortunate to have Alvis House, a much better halfway house than a county jail. I was fortunate after a few weeks to be granted home detention for the rest of my halfway house time. That occurred because I had a home, a job (at a local law firm), transportation, and a family support system. Most inmates are not as fortunate as my situation, and that awareness motivated me to become involved in organizations that help restored citizens return to the general population. That is where I learned the critical importance of three factors: ***jobs, transportation, and family support.*** Those three factors often determine whether inmates become contributing citizens in society or return to prison.

In one of those organizations, Kindway/Embark, I

Chapter Nine: Beyond Y2K

> I learned the one factor that surpasses all the other three —faith.

learned the one factor that surpasses all the other three—*faith*. Faith-based programs have low rates of recidivism; nonfaith-based programs often do not.

What I did not know when I left FCI Morgantown is that some people would welcome me back and some would not. I also did not fully understand that a felony conviction is a sentence for life, making it difficult to find employers who are not prejudiced against hiring restored citizens who have fully served their sentence. One of those who welcomed me was the Dean at the business school where I taught 40 years and hoped to return. She met with me at breakfast and told me about former students who commented about my teaching skills. "I have no doubt about your qualifications," she said, "but I won't hire you because I don't want to take phone calls from parents who will complain about having a felon in the classroom."

Although I could not return to the university I loved, I was fortunate to be offered a position at a prominent law firm, where I joined an office that welcomed me and my marketing experience.

Home Detention

Home detention is very detaining. Except for specific exceptions, I could not leave home even to jog around my neighborhood. Before leaving for work, I had to call the halfway house from home and report in as soon as I reached the office and repeat that process returning home at the end of day.

Home detention had three exceptions. One was one religious service per week for four hours. I wanted to split the four hours to church on Sunday morning and Bible study on Tuesday morning, but that was not allowed. The rule says ONE service per week, not two, even if both could be accomplished in four hours. The other exceptions are one shopping trip at a maximum of two hours per week and one restaurant visit per week at a maximum of two hours including travel time. That exception turned out to be the best thing that happened to me after prison.

The person responsible for marketing at the Ohio State Press was an intelligent lady named Linda who wrote me occasionally while I was at Morgantown. Her position at the Ohio State Press had responsibility for marketing books published by the Press, including *From the Edge of the World*, my first non-textbook book, which continued to sell well during my incarceration. Linda and I met before the prison stint, but I did not know her beyond one lunch we'd had before I left for Morgantown. Naturally, I wanted to meet her again and express my appreciation for the sales of my book while in prison.

Every restaurant visit had to be approved in advance by Alvis House along with the name of the other person attending, the name and phone number of the restaurant, and a strict requirement to call before leaving and after returning home. After explaining these rules to Linda, I sent an email asking if she would be available and interested in having dinner with me any night the week of February 12. She responded she would pick me up and deliver me back to my house (to minimize travel time in the two-hour limit) and was available on Tuesday of that week. Initially, I did not realize that Tuesday was February 14, but fortunately I did realize it before she arrived and had flowers for her. The rest

Chapter Nine: Beyond Y2K

is history and I am now married to Linda, the most wonderful wife anyone could ever have. God sometimes saves the best for last.

Life After Y2K

Prince wrote a song during the height of the Cold War about fears of a nuclear Armageddon, when the United States was stockpiling nuclear weapons and taking a strong stance against the Soviet Union. This scared a lot of people, especially when Prince voiced their concerns with the words "Everybody's got a bomb. We could all die any day." Prince was more optimistic, making the point that we should enjoy whatever time we have on earth while we still can, even if it all ends by the year 2000.

My life did not end in 2000, but good times started going wrong, starting with the sale of Worthington Foods in 1999, something I did not want to happen and did not vote for. I was serving on too many boards and attended most of the Worthington meetings by phone. When I went to the final meeting in person, I recognized other board members would probably vote to sell the company, so I asked our corporate attorney whether if a board member voted against the sale would increase the likelihood of a shareholder suit challenging the sale. He said yes and I concluded costs of a shareholder suit would reduce the amount shareholders would receive, so I abstained. One of my biggest regrets is that I did not aggressively oppose the sale of a company making meat substitutes that today would be a billion-dollar business. And I doubt there would have been a legal case against me if I had voted for what I believed was right instead of complying with the desires of other board members. Today, when I serve on private boards, I vote my conscience, not compliance with views of other board members. ***Not standing up for your beliefs to keep others happy, in the long run, undermines the ability of others to value your opinions.***

Until that momentous event at the turn of the century, most things had gone very well for me with ample awards for what I enjoyed most, teaching at Ohio State. I also enjoyed teaching executive programs, providing financial rewards several times my university salary. Boards on which I served also built ample resources for my eventual retirement.

Y2K began as a decade when both the U.S. and my personal economy were at all-time highs. By the end of that decade, both had collapsed, and I was sleeping on a steel plate as a bed and teaching inmates for $50 a month. At Ohio State, I enjoyed receiving teaching awards. There were no teaching awards in prison, only the reward of helping men reach for a better life. A decade after Y2K in a prison cell, I could not party like I did in 1999.

In his book *A Horse and His Boy*, C.S. Lewis wrote, "When things go wrong, you'll find they usually go on getting worse for some time; but when things once start going right, they often go on getting better and better."

Things did get worse throughout the Y2K decade. The million-dollar fine and millions of dollars in legal fees ravaged my retirement resources. My second marriage ended in divorce. I lost the job I loved at the zenith of my career. And, I went to prison.

In good times, I defended God, always ready to tell people reasons to believe in His existence. In prison I learned to depend on God, not just defend Him. There were people in prison who offered help, such as a man in the cell next to mine who told me had a shank hidden in his cell and said, "I got your back," but that is not the same security as the Holy

Chapter Nine: Beyond Y2K

Spirit "having your back." The Holy Spirit is as important for thriving in prison as oxygen is for surviving in life.

In prison you learn a lot about a nation and the justice system. I observed two former Congressmen explain how conference committees and politics really operate with more candor than any textbook or media account I have ever seen. One of my GED students who was a Mafia hit man told me he "hit 26 people, but none that didn't deserve it." He may have enforced fairer justice than a court system. I now understood what Nelson Mandela, who spent 23 more years in prison than I did, meant when he said, "No one understands a nation until he spends time in its prisons." I learned God goes through stormy waters with His followers. When you have met God personally and depend on His Son, Jesus Christ, you are never alone.

God goes through stormy waters with His followers. When you have met God personally and depend on His Son, Jesus Christ, you are never alone.

When my son picked me up in Morgantown and headed toward Columbus, as C.S. Lewis said, things started getting better and better. The end of prison was a new beginning for the rest of life.

The first breakthrough was an invitation to be visiting lecturer at Wheaton College, where I was warmly welcomed. Since I was still "on paper," my parole officer diligently sought permission for me to travel out of the Southern District of Ohio when I was still on supervised release. A few other invitations to lecture at universities and business groups started to happen.

The big breakthrough came, however, when I wrote a book on how to start and grow small businesses. The motivation came from teaching inmates and restored citizens how to get a job. Many times, I heard the response "Aww, Blackwell, no one will give me a job because I have a felony conviction."

My response was "You may be right, so give *yourself* a job by starting a business."

"I don't have any money and I don't know how" was often the response. I told them most successful businesses start with limited capital, and two-thirds of Forbes billionaires started with nothing or nearly nothing. I decided to write a book to give inmates and everyone else knowledge needed to start and grow a successful business.

When my literary agent showed the manuscript to publishers, including some who published my previous books, the answer from all was "We can't hire a felon as an author about business." But "by chance" I was at a meeting where Christian author Richard Simmons was speaking. I met one of his executives from Union Hill Publishing in Birmingham who agreed to look at the manuscript. It was not long before they published my first book since prison, *Saving America: How Garage Entrepreneurs Grow Small Firms into Large Fortunes*. It relaunched my teaching career to executive groups, first in Ohio and eventually all over the nation, an activity that currently occupies most of my time.

Roger's Rules for Success, something I formed long before Y2K, was a collection of guiding principles in my career. In prison, they became principles for survival. They are mostly truths I learned from the example of my parents, who were better parents than I am, from professors, and from many of the 65,000 students in my classes. I also believe each of *Roger's Rules* is firmly rooted in biblical principles. They are

Chapter Nine: Beyond Y2K

printed on the next page in the hope they will encourage you to write your own Rules for Success. Yours will probably be different than mine, and that is fine. If you are a parent, you may want to involve your children in writing and living them.

These rules helped me teach future business leaders in careers where success is measured with basic principles such as ROI (Return on Investment), ROA (Return on Assets), and ARR (Annual Recurring Revenue). Along the way I learned the most important principle is measured in ERR (Eternal Rate of Return).

When Y2K began, I had fame and fortune far beyond anything I planned or aspired to achieve, but both mostly vanished in the decade that followed. Prison is a humbling experience. But through it all, God went with me, often in miraculous ways. I learned that *fame and fortune tempt people to put Self on the throne of life, leaving God only with what is left*. I hope you will not need to go to prison to learn that lesson. It is a lesson that lasts not just for a century, but for eternity.

ROGER'S RULES FOR SUCCESS

- Treat every individual you meet with respect and kindness.
- When individuals treat you with unkindness or lack of respect, reread Rule #1.
- Help as many people as you can, in as many ways as you can, for as long as you can.
- If you cannot say something good about someone, say nothing about that person at all.
- Love your work. Successful people work for more than for what they are paid.
- Be frugal. Save for the rainy day because rainy days always occur. What you have is determined more by what you save than what you earn.
- Make difficult decisions based on long-term effects rather than immediate gratification. Live to learn, learn to live.
- Eat healthy, and exercise regularly. You will live longer, spend less, and be happier.
- Lasting success is derived from finding out what God wants you to do and then doing it.
- Love conquers everything else.

—*Roger Blackwell*

Roger's Rules for Success was given to thousands of students and to audiences where he spoke. Roger has received messages from people saying they posted these rules on corporate bulletin boards, dormitory walls, government offices, military barracks, and prison cells. Feel free to print a copy to use in your life or organization.

www.rogerblackwellbusiness.com

CHAPTER TEN

Take My Hand

WHEN TEACHING the Death and Dying class at Ohio State, sometimes I included a trick question on the exam: "True or False: The mortality rate for males is higher than females." The correct answer is false.

The mortality rate of both males and females is 100 percent. It is also 100 percent for every race, religion, or national origin. For people age 20 or age 100, the mortality rate is 100 percent. News stories often report mortality rates associated with smoking, alcohol, or other risks. More careful interpretations report the number of *premature* deaths. The event that always causes death is birth. Other risks and events determine the *timing* of death.

The more people understand and face death, the better prepared they are to live. The first chapter of this book was about birth, and middle chapters described events during life, so it seems appropriate the last chapter should be about death. You might escape taxes by hiring a new accountant or changing your residence, but no one escapes death.

Understanding the inevitability of death does not diminish pain and sorrow when it happens. For me, the most painful period in prison was the death of my mother. Her death was foreseeable when I entered Morgantown because of her diabetes and relentless progression of Alzheimer's in the years before prison. It was still a shock when notification arrived of her death about a year after entering Morgantown.

Fellow inmates receiving furloughs to attend a funeral gave me advice about how to request permission. The CO who handled my case was cooperative and immediately submitted a request through channels to secure approval of the Warden and others whose permission was required. Since I had not yet achieved "out" status allowing temporary departure, I needed to pay for an armed guard to accompany me. My son immediately deposited funds to pay for the guard. My son and I also discussed a time for the service that would allow leaving the prison early morning, drive to Columbus with the guard, and return for the evening count. Everything was approved by the Bureau of Prisons for me to attend.

Two days before the service, the manager of my housing unit called me to his office and said when the court in Columbus discovered the prison was going to grant me a furlough to attend the funeral, the court ordered the BOP to stop my departure. Once again, I discovered the meaning of Nelson Mandela's comment that no one understands a nation's "justice" until they spend time in its prisons. I also understood once again the unlimited authority of a Federal Judge. The unit manager apologized and expressed his sympathy. I returned to my cell to cry alone.

Throughout this book, you read about my birth, the train escape, and a serious medical issue in prison, but those were only a few of the times death lurked but was delayed. I could

Chapter Ten: Take My Hand

also have written about God's intervention in perilous places such as Medellin, Columbia, townships in Africa, Nablus, and the Gaza Strip in Israel and Lima, Peru, where I was mugged by young men with knives. Most people thought I travelled alone to those places. But I did not. God had his eye on me, even if no one else did.

In the Jewish scriptures, when God asked Moses to lead the people of Israel out of Egypt, Moses said to God, "Suppose I go to the people of Israel and they ask who sent me? God answered Moses and said, "I Am Who I Am." Jesus said something similar when He was asked His identity. Rabbis sometimes say the best interpretation of God's name is Hebrew for "He was, he is, and he will be." In rabbinic interpretation, God's name reflects the three tenses: past, present, and future. I have read Hebrew scholars who interpret "I AM" not only as plural ("we") but as "the One who will go through it with my people."

God said that to Moses when facing the Red Sea in front of him and Egyptian chariots chasing him from behind. That description of God made sense to me in prison—God is the One Who will go through it with you. There is also a future tense when thinking about God, captured in lyrics by Tommy A. Dorsey.

Dorsey was the son of a Baptist preacher; his mother was the church organist. Through many problems in his youth, he struggled between the secular and the sacred but eventually wrote hundreds of Gospel songs. The one for which he is most famous is Take My Hand, with the following lyrics.

Precious Lord, take my hand
Lead me on, let me stand
I'm tired, I'm weak, I'm lone
Through the storm, through the night

YOU ARE NOT ALONE

Lead me on to the light
Take my hand, precious Lord, lead me home

That song comforted me the day Mother's service occurred and I was not allowed to attend. I hope that song will be sung, perhaps accompanied by a trumpet, at my own service, which I know will happen long before Y3K. As I move closer to that time, I think of a passage in I Corinthians describing life as a race. If I had known the plan God had for my life when it began, I do not know whether I would have said yes to the plan or not, but God knew details I never could have imagined. Although I stumbled many times along the way, I enjoyed the race!

My mother and my father "crossed over Jordan's River," as gospel songs describe what happens after death. Someday it will happen to me, as surely as the day I left Morgantown. Someday it will happen to you and everyone who reaches out for His hand.

Hopefully, you discerned as you read these pages the influences of Mother and Father. When writing this book, I thought about how I might summarize how their life shaped mine. I decided the best way was to print the eulogy I wrote in prison for my Mother's service but was not allowed to attend and the eulogy for my Father, written very soon after my release from FCI Morgantown.

Both eulogies are reprinted exactly as they were written in the hope you can discern from their lives examples of faith that will be helpful for the rest of your life.

Chapter Ten: Take My Hand

**Eulogy for Rheva Allen Blackwell
(October 13, 1914 - February 19, 2007)
Written by Roger Blackwell and read at her Memorial
Service by her grandson, Christian Blackwell**

Few people live their life entirely for others. My mother was one who did. Most people work hard to obtain an education with degrees that recognize their achievements. Mother worked hard to be sure her husband and her son received their education rather than her own. She was proud of their degrees, with no remorse that they obtained degrees instead of her.

If there were flowers to be grown and arranged on the tables of church dinners, Mother did that. She did that hundreds of times, not for recognition but as a service of beauty to God. If anyone tried to count how many cookies she baked to give to others, they would have lost count long ago. Whether they were for friends, the GA's at church, or her grandchildren, she baked cookies for the pleasure of others. That was the story of her life.

Anyone who has success as a writer does so partly because of their success as a reader. Often, the reason for reading ability can be found in the lap of a parent reading books to small children. It was that way for me. Some of my earliest memories of Mother are from the years we were on a farm near the tiny town of King City, Missouri. Before I entered first grade, Mother read to me until covers were tattered and the books were falling apart. These books always included Bible stories of Joshua fighting the battle of Jericho, Jonah and the whale, and Joseph with his coat of many colors. She read those books to me repeatedly, with little recognition for her service in teaching me to read, perhaps until this moment.

I wish I had thanked her more often.

If I have achieved success as a teacher, I probably owe that to my father. But my success in business, I owe to my mother. When I was eight years old, Mother said, "Would you like a job?" I said, "That sounds like fun!" With Mother's help, we sent away for a sample kit from the New England Greeting Card Company. I quickly sold the samples and ordered more. By the time I was in high school, Mother had shown me how to build a business generating several thousand dollars a year with as much profit as some adults were making at that time. Nearly everything I needed to know about consumer behavior, I learned from my mother in the operation of that greeting card business.

Today, it is not unusual for women to receive recognition for their success in business, sometimes as CEOs of major corporations. Some people may not know that my mother was the CEO of Teachers Credit Union in Warrensburg, Missouri. She took a small, struggling, nearly defunct business and built it into a million-dollar business. She did it not for recognition; she did it to support her family with a husband who had just barely survived death from a heart attack. What women do today, often receiving prestige and acclaim, Mother did in service to her family.

She never received accolades for her business skills, though they were many; she never received awards for her flower arrangements, although they were award-worthy, nor for her creative cookies and cooking skills. She never received degrees for her education even though she was as intelligent, or more so, than either of the two men in her life for whom she lived. My mother's life was a life of love and service to others, especially her husband and her "one and only" son, as she always referred to me.

Many women want recognition for their roles as a mother and wife. I never observed Mother seeking such recognition, but I know the pleasure she received from the accomplishments of her husband and her son. Their successes were always foremost for her, with no apparent desire for recognition of her own activities, as important and skillful as they were.

Many people have heard my father tell the story of my birth. They know that I was still-born, set aside as dead and deprived of oxygen for many minutes. My father and my grandmother

Chapter Ten: Take My Hand

caressed me back to life while the doctor and nurse struggled desperately to keep Mother alive. Even in my birth, my mother nearly gave her life for me.

I recently read a helpful statement by the French scientist and philosopher Pascal. He observed, "Be we heroic as we like, the end awaits the noblest life in the world. Let us reflect on this, that there is no good in this life except in the hope of another. We are happy only in proportion as we draw near it, as there are no more woes for those who have complete assurance of eternity."

My mother had complete assurance of her eternity. So, also can we have complete assurance of her happiness today. Each of us here today will also have happiness the closer we draw near to that same eternity. Pascal added one more truth, saying, "There is no happiness for them who have no insight into eternity." If you hear or read these words about my mother and have no assurance of your eternity in God's presence, where she now is, there is no better time than today to decide about your own eternity. Confess with your lips and believe in your heart that Jesus Christ is the Son of God, raised from the dead for the sins of each of us, and you will achieve that assurance.

My mother is experiencing happiness with God in Heaven. Each of us gathered here today honor her memory; we can also be assured of that eternity. Many people live a life of prosperity, achievement, and recognition. My mother lived a life of service to others: mostly to her husband and her son, but also to her church, to her friends and family, and always to God, in Whose presence she now dwells.

Thank you, Mother, for the life you gave for Christian and Rebecca Rheva, whom you loved almost as much as my father and me, and for Josie, Lindy, and Jude, whom you did not have as much time to know as well as we all would have liked.

Thank you, Mother, for a life of service to others.

Your "one and only" son, Roger

YOU ARE NOT ALONE

Eulogy for Dale Joseph Blackwell
(April 14, 1915 - May 14, 2011)
Written and read by Roger Dale Blackwell at his father's Memorial Service

Young people and all people need heroes, men and women, as role models to shape and guide our lives. Two of my heroes are Billy Graham and Peter Drucker. Billy Graham has probably introduced more people to an eternity of Heaven than anyone since St. Paul, always with an impeccable personal life. Peter Drucker was a business professor's professor, a consummate consultant serving as an exemplary role model for anyone who aspires to both professions. But as great as these two men were, neither is as influential nor more of a hero in my eyes as my father.

Starting from humble beginnings as a farm boy in the poorest county of Missouri, he accomplished success in everything he did. It took him 13 years to get his undergraduate degree, going to the university in summers and teaching in a rural school the rest of the year, but time and poverty did not stop him at the undergraduate degree. He persevered until he received two master's degrees— in Accounting and Education—and a doctorate in Business and Education. When he wrote his doctoral dissertation, I was in high school and had the great privilege of typing it for him.

Some of you may not know that he helped people start or grow several businesses. He involved me in some of those, including every phase of starting a new radio station in Maryville, Missouri. Years later, when he was no longer involved, I became Chief Engineer of that station.

Most of the passion I inherited for teaching was not a matter of genetics as much as observing how much he cared about students. When he experienced a heart attack, I remember a young African-American visiting him telling me how much he respected

Chapter Ten: Take My Hand

my father. I asked what my Dad did that was so special for him. "Nothing," he answered, "except treat me like everyone else. Not many people do that."

Some of Dad's greatest admirers were students from Hindu, Islamic, and other backgrounds, and because of his great concern for them, they often reciprocated by inviting him to a meal in their home and accepting an invitation to visit his church.

The greatest reason for respecting my father is his love of family. Not just my mother and me and his grandchildren, but all his family. He truly loved his sisters and his brother and all their children. Not many people stay married to the same person for 73 years, and not just married, but in love with my mother for eternity. I should have paid more attention to that lesson.

In all my life, I never heard my father utter a profanity of any kind, nor did I ever hear him say an unkind word about anyone. The only times I saw my dad angry was when someone took advantage of other people, but never to the point of losing his composure or doing anything except try to correct injustice when he observed it. He never smoked, never cursed, never drank nor gambled, and he never spent money foolishly.

I also never saw him fail to help someone who needed help, whether in the form of food or money, physical assistance, or simply someone to listen and give practical advice. Whether it was alcohol, foolish decisions about money, or any other of the maladies of life, Dad did not give up on people with problems. I never saw him show deference to people because of their wealth or influence, nor ignore someone because they were limited or poor. He treated everyone the same—with care, concern, and compassion.

In a book by Os Guiness, The Call, *Ernest Becker describes a great human being as "A man who lives in faith, who has given over the meaning of his life to his Creator, and who lives centered on the energies of his Creator. He accepts whatever happens in this visible dimension without complaint, lives his life as a duty, faces his death without a qualm. No pettiness is so petty that it threatens his meaning; no task is too frightening to be beyond his courage. He is fully in the world on its terms and wholly beyond the world in his trust in the invisible dimension."*

Dad knew that invisible dimension was revealed in the Word of God. Dad listened to God's call and walked, and in his last years rolled, with God.

My father lived so close to God that when his time came, he had only a short step home, or for Dad, a short roll in his power wheelchair.

Dad lived not because he had anything to prove, nor for any others to approve. He had nothing to gain, or lose, except to do what God called him to do—live a life of faithfulness for 73 years to his high school sweetheart, to be a teacher, counselor, and inspiration to thousands of students ranging from first-graders in a one-room rural school to professor in major universities, and most of all, a strong and dependable beacon of love for his only son, his grandchildren, and great-grandchildren, his sisters and brother and their children, and for decades of church members ranging from the little church that baptized him in a nearby river many years ago to churches in Missouri and here in Columbus in which he served as deacon, confidant, and stalwart supporter for decades.

I'll close by reading an email I received last Saturday from a close friend in the Netherlands, not many hours after my father died. It said:

'Dear Roger, the world became much poorer today because it lost the nicest man I ever met in my life: your father. He was very special for our family. It was always a pleasure to visit him. He was able to awake the good things in me. He uplifted me. He taught me a lot and I have learned a lot from him. He was like a father for me; I will miss him very much. We know your father's *condition became poor more and more the last years. He suffered from missing your mother and missing you, but he was always positive and hopeful. I never heard a bad thing out of his mouth. He was also a strong believer and we know that he will have a better life now. But we also know that you, Christian, Frances and the great-grandchildren will miss him.*

When Jannie and I said goodbye to him last year he told us that there was only one good reason for him to live longer and that was to see you again. We thank God that that strong wish of his has been fulfilled.'

I know that many of you here today prayed he would live until I returned home. I thank each of you for those prayers and the many ways you helped him and me until my return. Those prayers were answered. Thank you."

CONCLUSION

You Are Not Alone

"HIS EYE is on the sparrow. I know He watches me." You have probably heard that song many times, perhaps by Ethel Waters, Whitney Houston, or the favorite singer of Dr. Martin Luther King (and my personal favorite), Mahalia Jackson. The song was written over 100 years ago by Civilla D. Martin and Charles H. Gabriel, inspired by the words of Jesus in the book of Matthew: "Look at the birds of the air; they neither sow nor reap nor gather into barns, and yet your heavenly Father feeds them."

The sparrow is important in both the song and in the Bible passage because it symbolizes power even in a creature of small, insignificant size. The sparrow represents hard work, diligence, productivity, and persistence, lessons I learned from my parents that you hopefully observed throughout this book. In ancient cultures, the sparrow was often a symbol of joy, friendship, and teamwork. Like peasants oppressed by powerful people, the sparrow survived even though surrounded by big and dangerous animals such as lions, bears,

Look at the birds of the air; they neither sow nor reap nor gather into barns and yet your heavenly Father feeds them.

Matthew 6:26

and wolves. Somehow, against all dangers and suffering, sparrows survive because of God's care for them.

Do you think sparrows are aware God's eye is on them? That seems unlikely for the sparrow but also for many ordinary people like you and me. Some people move through life, sometimes with danger and suffering instead of prosperity and pleasure, unaware that God has his eye on them in good times and bad. God's own name for Himself is "I AM"—the One who goes through life with you, whether that journey takes you through green pastures, the Red Sea chased by Egyptian chariots or a painful prison.

I am confident that some of you reading this book are reading it while in prison. If so, you know prisoners cannot release themselves. Only the government can do that. But if you have learned by faith that God is going through prison with you, you also know you can depend on Him to meet you on the other side of R&D.

If you are reading this book in prison, you can trust God to lead you out the gate to a more fulfilling life here until he leads you to a permanent life with Him in Heaven, where he has a mansion prepared for you.

You may be one of the many without faith or whose faith is in something or someone other than God. Perhaps you believe God is unavailable or unapproachable and have never discovered His eye is on you. If that is your situation, it is never too late to make that discovery and establish a personal relationship with Him through Jesus Christ. Jesus knocks at the door of your heart and soul but he does not kick down the door like the police sometimes do. He waits for you to open the door to your soul and invite Him into your life. Faith is not just a noun; it is also a verb.

If you are like most people reading this book, you are not reading it in prison. If that is true, you might want to take a moment to stop reading and give thanks you are not in prison. Criminologists in a position to know who is guilty and who is not guilty believe about 30 percent of people in prison are not guilty, whether they are a victim of the justice system or simply a decision that a plea was less costly than a defense. Prison could happen to anyone, including you, so be thankful you are not in prison. Many lives have been transformed spiritually while in prison by such notables as Aleksandr Solzhenitsyn, but you can learn to depend on God without going to prison!

It is likely, however, that every reader of this book has experienced pain and suffering. If you have not already, you will. Cancer is worse than prison. So is the death of a child, a serious debilitating illness, a pandemic, and sometimes divorce or loss of job. The death rate for both men and women is 100%. To be human is to suffer. If you have travelled through any of these, you know how helpful it is

God's own name for Himself is "I AM"— the One who goes through life with you, whether that journey takes you through green pastures, the Red Sea chased by Egyptian chariots or a painful prison.

to know God goes through the suffering alongside you. If you have not established that relationship, perhaps you have avoided such a decision, thinking it was not the right time. Maybe this is the right time.

In the book *More Beautiful than Before: How Suffering Transforms Us*, Rabbi Steve Leder relates a Marshall McLuhan saying: "We don't know who discovered water, but it wasn't the fish." Levin then describes what happens when you take a fish out of water, whether by hook or by net. Gasping and flailing for breath, the fish discovers what happens to a fish without water. I recommend that book, and so does Pastor Rick Warren, author of *Purpose Driven Life*, for its many insights into suffering, but the insight I encourage you to consider is discovering water before you are suddenly without it. The living water that Jesus describes is the Holy Spirit, and the way to receive Living Water is through a personal relationship with God. Do not wait until you are like a fish out of water to discover what it means to be a follower of Jesus, the Messiah.

You may be living a life as comfortable as I was pre-Y2K, but my favorite business author, Peter Drucker, says, "If you are comfortable, it's a sure sign you are doing things wrong." Fortunately, when I was dragged from the comfort of a professor's life into the discomfort of prison, I was fortunate to have the Source of Living Water go with me.

Maybe you read this book knowing I was a Christian. If so, I hope you found assurance that whatever your future, you are not alone. If you read the book for some other reason, it is appropriate that I ask you to consider how you answer the question "Does God exist?" You don't have to be a Bayesian statistician to consider that a relevant question, but if you want a logical, factual analysis of faith, I encourage you to read such classic books as C.S. Lewis' *Mere Christianity*

Conclusion: You Are Not Alone

or Tim Keller's *The Reason for God* for solid, fact-base evidence or the very recent book by Richard E. Simmons III, *Reflections on the Existence of God*. You will find these sources full of evidence for the existence of God, but through personal dependence on Him in good times and bad, it would be easier to convince me the sun will rise in the West tomorrow morning than believing God does not exist.

As a researcher and professor, I spent much of my time encouraging graduate students to search the source materials in any critical analysis of an important issue, and no issue is more important than your relationship to God. The source material about that subject also has a name: *The Holy Bible*.

Sometimes people say, "I would like to examine the Bible, but it is long, and I don't know where to begin." Sometimes people read a few chapters of the first book, Genesis, and get bogged down in names and events that are not always easy to understand without background knowledge.

My suggestion is you turn to the last part of the Bible called the New Testament and look for the book of John. You will find it after books called Matthew, Mark, and Luke. Those are names you may have read or at least heard someone read at Christmas. The next book in that series, called the Gospels, is John. It is the easiest place to start and summarizes the other Gospels and the rest of the Bible. A lot of homes and some hotel rooms still have Bibles, but if not, I am sure you will find one in any library, bookstore, or church. Amazon has many translations in many languages.

In John, you will find the favorite verse of sports fans. At least it seems to be the favorite verse because you see it at almost every sports event on signs inscribed as John 3:16. "For God so loved the world that he gave his one and only Son, that whoever believes in him may have eternal life."

John 3 also describes how Nicodemus, one of the important Jewish leaders when Jesus walked on earth, came to Jesus at night asking the question "Rabbi, we know you couldn't be doing the things you are doing if God was not with you. What must I do to enter the Kingdom of God?" The answer to Nicodemus and to everyone since then was to be born again of water and the Spirit. And everyone who does that, Jesus promised, shall not perish but have eternal life. Read the rest of the book of John for details.

When I was teaching the death course at Ohio State, sometimes students would express great concern about a problem. "If I don't pass this course, I won't be able to graduate" was sometimes the plea. To which I sometimes responded, "What if you don't graduate?" They might answer, "Then I wouldn't be able to get a job." That is not literally true, of course, but I then extended their thinking by saying "If you do not get a job, you might starve, and if you starve, you will die. But if you recognize the death rate is 100% for everyone, you already know you and everyone else will die. So, let's concentrate on what you need to do now. And by the way, if you invite him, God will go with you through the rest of your life until your final day, with his hand extended to welcome you on the other side."

God graciously extends a personal invitation to know Him through His Son Jesus. Do you know how? Have you made the decision to invite Jesus into your life? It is not complicated. Many have found the answer to the most important question in life in a prayer proclaimed around the world by Dr. Billy Graham.

> "Dear Lord Jesus, I know I am a sinner and ask for your forgiveness. I believe you died for my sins and rose from the dead. I turn from my sins and invite you

Conclusion: You Are Not Alone

Ask Jesus to take control of your life, acknowledge you have made and will make mistakes for which you need His forgiveness. If you do that ... you will discover you are not alone whatever the future has in store for you.

to come into my heart and life. I want to trust and follow you as my Lord and Savior. Amen."

Congratulations! According to God's word in Romans 10:9-10 if you confess with your mouth "Jesus is Lord and believe in your heart that God raised him from the dead, you will be saved. For it is with your heart that you believe and are justified, and it is with your mouth that you confess and are saved."

It is an unconditional promise that all your sins—past, present, and future—are paid for. In addition to His presence in your life now, it means you are established as a *permanent resident of Heaven*. That is great news!

The plan to bridge the chasm between God and people such as you and me is straightforward. Ask Jesus to take control of your life, acknowledge you have made and will make mistakes for which you need His forgiveness. If you do that (right now if you have not already made that decision), you will discover you are not alone whatever the future has in store for you. The future may include good times and certainly will include some bad times, but through it all, I learned to trust in Jesus. I hope you do also. You will discover wherever you go and whatever you do, you are not alone.

YOU ARE NOT ALONE

If you have made that decision, see you in Heaven! If I get there before you, tell me about reading this book when you look me up in Heaven (probably not far from my parents). And you might want to bring some friends with you.